WARRIOR • 138

ROOSEVELT'S ROUGH RIDERS

ALEJANDRO DE QUESADA ILLUSTRATED BY STEPHEN WALSH

Series editors Marcus Cowper and Nikolai Bogdanovic

First published in 2009 by Osprey Publishing

Midland House, West Way, Botley, Oxford OX2 0PH, UK

44-02 23rd St, Suite 219, Long Island City, NY 11101, USA

E-mail: info@ospreypublishing.com

A CIP catalog record for this book is available from the British Library.

ISBN: 978 1 84603 383 4

E-Book ISBN: 978 1 84603 904 1

Editorial by Ilios Publishing Ltd, Oxford UK (www.iliospublishing.com)

Page layouts and origination by PDQ Media, UK

Index by Mike Parkin

Typeset in Sabon and Myriad Pro

Printed in China through Worldprint Ltd

10 11 12 13 12 10 9 8 7 6 5 4 3 2

FOR A CATALOG OF ALL BOOKS PUBLISHED BY OSPREY MILITARY AND AVIATION PLEASE CONTACT:

Osprey Direct, c/o Random House Distribution Center,
400 Hahn Road, Westminster, MD 21157
E-mail: uscustomerservice@ospreypublishing.com

Osprey Direct, The Book Service Ltd, Distribution Centre,
Colchester Road, Frating Green, Colchester, Essex, CO7 7DW
E-mail: customerservice@ospreypublishing.com

www.ospreypublishing.com

ARTIST'S NOTE

Readers may care to note that the original paintings from which the color plates in this book were prepared are available for private sale. All reproduction copyright whatsoever is retained by the Publishers. All enquiries should be addressed to:

Mr Stephen Walsh, 11 Longacre St, Macclesfield, Cheshire, SK10 1AY, UK

The Publishers regret that they can enter into no correspondence upon this matter.

THE WOODLAND TRUST

Osprey Publishing are supporting the Woodland Trust, the UK's leading woodland conservation charity, by funding the dedication of trees.

ACKNOWLEDGMENTS

I would like to thank the following individuals, societies, and museums that made this work possible: Mark Kasal, John Langellier, Pietro "Pete" Scarafiotti, Myers Brown, Alex Solera, Ron G. Hickox, Mike Lewis, Fred Wardinsky, Ed DeLaire, Dave White, The Company of Military Historians, National Archives, Library of Congress, Theodore Roosevelt's Birthplace National Historic Site (National Park Service), The Henry B. Plant Museum, Jefferson Barracks, and AdeQ Historical Archives.

CONTENTS

ROOSEVELT'S ROUGH RIDERS

INTRODUCTION

Of all the units from American military history, the 1st United States Volunteer Cavalry Regiment, otherwise known as the "Rough Riders," has become the most recognizable entity in American culture. Sports teams are named after them, and local schools are named after those who served such as Theodore Roosevelt, Leonard Wood, and Bucky O'Neill. These men were idolized in the

decades that followed their charge up that blood-soaked hill in Cuba during the hot summer of 1898. One became military governor of Cuba, another became president of the United States of America, and others still made their impact back home upon their return. However, most just blended into the American landscape, never to be heard from again.

What kind of men were they? Where did they come from? What brought them together from different walks of life? While most works on the Rough Riders concentrate on their role as a unit during the Spanish-American War, this work will attempt to explore what made these men into our modern-day vision of what a Rough Rider was – a symbol of rugged toughness, with a can-do attitude, and a patriotic zeal that defines the American Spirit of the early 20th century.

While it is easy to fall into the trap of judging a people of the past by current standards, one must remember that Theodore Roosevelt and his "Rough Riders" were products of their time. This work will focus on the actual characters of the Rough Riders through the writings of their members. The diaries, memoirs (such as Theodore Roosevelt's *The Rough Riders*), letters (such as those of Private Alexander H. Wallace), and newspaper accounts show glimpses of their lives and experiences during the Spanish-American War, as well as answering the questions highlighted above, and create a fuller picture of what it was like to be a Rough Rider.

CHRONOLOGY

February 24, 1895	Third Cuban Insurrection begins.
January 1, 1898	Spain institutes limited political autonomy in Cuba.
January 12, 1898	Spanish in Cuba "riot" or demonstrate against autonomy-supporting newspaper offices. Consul-General Lee takes this as a threat against Americans.
January 17, 1898	Consul-General Lee asks for a ship to be sent to Havana.
January 24, 1898	The battleship USS *Maine* is sent to Havana, arriving there the following day.
February 15, 1898	The USS *Maine* explodes in Havana Harbor, killing 266 Americans. Spain is blamed for the atrocity.
February 25, 1898	Theodore Roosevelt, Assistant Secretary of the Navy, cables Commodore Dewey to prepare his forces for war, and gives him his objectives.
April 11, 1898	President McKinley requests from Congress the power to interfere in Cuban affairs.
April 19, 1898	US Congress declares Cuba independent.
April 22, 1898	The blockade of Cuba is commenced by the US Navy. The first Spanish ship is taken.

April 22, 1898	US Congress passes the Volunteer Army Act calling for a volunteer cavalry of three regiments. Congress authorizes the creation of the 1st United States Volunteer Cavalry, popularly known as the "Rough Riders." In the course of the month they assemble in San Antonio to undergo intensive training.
April 23, 1898	Spain declares war on the United States.
April 25, 1898	President McKinley calls for volunteers to supplement the depleted army.
April 25, 1898	US declares war, but makes the declaration retroactive to April 22. Matanzas, Cuba is bombarded by the US Navy.
April 27, 1898	Commodore Dewey's squadron leaves Mirs Bay, China for the Philippines.
April 30, 1898	Admiral Cervera's Spanish squadron leaves the Cape Verde Islands for the Caribbean.
May 1, 1898	The US Navy's Asiatic Squadron under Commodore Dewey defeats the Spanish Pacific Squadron at the Battle of Manila Bay.
May 6, 1898	Theodore Roosevelt resigns as assistant secretary of the Navy to become a lieutenant colonel of the 1st US Volunteer Cavalry Regiment.

"The other Rough Riders": Colonel Jay L. Torrey of the 2nd United States Volunteer Cavalry ("Torrey's Rough Riders")—one of three "Cowboy" cavalry regiments. Only Roosevelt's Rough Riders saw action during the war. (AdeQHA)

May 15, 1898	Theodore Roosevelt begins training with the Rough Riders.
May 26, 1898	The United States learns that the Spanish fleet is in Santiago Harbor in Cuba.
May 29, 1898	The US Navy blockades the Spanish fleet in Santiago Harbor.
June 14, 1898	The Rough Riders, now in Tampa, embark for Cuba on the SS *Yucatan*.
June 22, 1898	The Rough Riders arrive near Santiago.
June 24, 1898	The Battle of Las Guásimas. Lieutenant Colonel Roosevelt is promoted to colonel, as Colonel Wood is promoted to general in order to command a brigade.
July 1, 1898	The Battle of San Juan Heights and El Caney.
July 3, 1898	The Spanish fleet is destroyed outside Santiago de Cuba.
July 16, 1898	Spain signs the article of surrender.
July 17, 1898	The Spanish garrison in Santiago de Cuba capitulates.
August 6, 1898	The Rough Riders return to the United States aboard the SS *Miami*.

ABOVE LEFT
Even when in uniform, the Rough Riders still maintained their "western look." Note this figure's western-style saddle and pistol belt with holster for his Colt Single Action Army Revolver. (AdeQHA)

ABOVE RIGHT
Roosevelt's uniform was tailored by Brooks Brothers of New York. Upon his return to New York Colonel Roosevelt had a series of photographs taken of him in his well-used campaign uniform. This rare image show Roosevelt's complete set of collar insignia consisting of "U.S.V," Cavalry crossed sabers, and the US coat of arms badge. The latter is rarely seen since it appears behind the wearer's neck. Note the application of the colonel's shoulder straps over his epaulets. Roosevelt had pinned his battered hat's brim with the regimental cavalry insignia upon his return from Cuba. (AdeQHA)

August 14, 1898	The Rough Riders land at Montauk, Long Island, to begin a six-week quarantine.
September 13, 1898	The Rough Riders are mustered out of service; Spanish senate approves peace protocol.
September 27, 1898	Theodore Roosevelt is nominated by the Republican Party for the position of governor of New York State.
October 5, 1898	Roosevelt opens his governorship campaign at Carnegie Music Hall, and gives his speech on "the duties of a great nation."
October 17, 1898	Beginning of Theodore Roosevelt's New York State campaign tour, on which he is accompanied by uniformed Rough Riders. One blows a cavalry charge on a bugle before each speech.
November 8, 1898	Theodore Roosevelt is elected governor of New York State (661,715 votes) with a plurality of 17,786 votes, beating his Democrat opponent Augustus van Wyck of Brooklyn (643,921 votes).
December 10, 1898	The Treaty of Paris is signed by the US and Spain to end the Spanish-American War.
December 31, 1898	Theodore Roosevelt takes the oath of office before Secretary of State John Palmer.
January 1899	Roosevelt publishes *The Rough Riders*. The first instalment appears in *Scribner's Magazine* in January.
January 2, 1899	Governor Roosevelt's inauguration takes place.
February 2, 1899	Election of Theodore Roosevelt as commander of the Naval and Military Order of the Spanish-American War.
February 4, 1899	The Philippine Insurrection under General Emilio Aguinaldo begins.
June 24–25, 1899	The Rough Riders' first reunion is held in Las Vegas, Nevada.
May 31, 1900	The Rough Riders' dinner is held at Union League Club, New York City.
June 21, 1900	Roosevelt is nominated for vice president at the Republican National Convention, as running mate to President William McKinley, Philadelphia, Pennsylvania.
November 6, 1900	Theodore Roosevelt is elected vice president. The McKinley–Roosevelt ticket receives 7,219,530 votes to 6,358,071 for the Democrats William Jennings Bryan and Adlai E. Stevenson.

March 4, 1901	McKinley's second inauguration takes place, with Roosevelt inaugurated as vice-president.
March 23, 1901	The Philippine Revolutionary leader General Aguinaldo is captured.
September 14, 1901	McKinley dies after being shot on September 6. Theodore Roosevelt becomes president.
July 4, 1902	Roosevelt declares the Philippines pacified.
November 8, 1904	Roosevelt is elected president over Alton B. Parker, the Democratic nominee, by the widest popular margin ever recorded.
March 4, 1905	Theodore Roosevelt is inaugurated as president (second term).
March 4, 1909	Roosevelt retires from the presidency, being succeeded by William Howard Taft.
January 6, 1919	Roosevelt dies at Sagamore Hill; his death is caused by an arterial blood clot.
June 29, 1975	Jesse Langdon, the last surviving member of the Rough Riders and the only one to attend the final two reunions, in 1967 and 1968, dies at the age of 94.
January 16, 2001	Theodore Roosevelt becomes the first president to posthumously receive the Medal of Honor, the highest award for military service given in the United States, for his actions during the Battle of San Juan Hill.

Regimental staff wearing a variety of uniforms from the enlisted men/NCOs including the M1883 blouse and M1884 fatigue uniform. The officers are wearing either the M1898 or modified M1884 fatigue uniforms. One officer, at center, is wearing the M1895 officers' fatigue coat. (AdeQHA)

RECRUITMENT AND ENLISTMENT

Recruiting

The men that made up the 1st United States Volunteer Cavalry came from all walks of life, which made the regiment the most unique military unit in American history. Although Congress authorized the establishment of three volunteer cavalry regiments from the west, only the first regiment would see combat and gain fame. The regiment was mustered in between May 1 and May 21, 1898, at stations in the Indian Territory (today's State of Oklahoma), Texas, Montana, and New Mexico Territory. Colonel Roosevelt explained the problems in raising the regiment in his memoirs *The Rough Riders*:

> The difficulty in organizing was not in selecting, but in rejecting men. Within a day or two after it was announced that we were to raise the regiment, we were literally deluged with applications from every quarter of the Union. Without the slightest trouble, so far as men went, we could have raised a brigade or even a division … It was impossible to take any of the numerous companies which were proffered to us from the various States. The only organized bodies we were at liberty to accept were those from the four Territories. But owing to the fact that the number of men originally allotted to us, 780, was speedily raised to 1,000, we were given a chance to accept quite a number of eager volunteers who did not come from the Territories, but who possessed precisely the same temper that distinguished our Southwestern recruits, and whose presence materially benefited the regiment.

The men from the southwest were particularly what Theodore Roosevelt was looking for in raising the regiment:

> They were a splendid set of men, these Southwesterners—tall and sinewy, with resolute, weather-beaten faces, and eyes that looked a man straight in the face without flinching. They included in their ranks men of every occupation; but the three types were those of the cow-boy, the hunter, and the mining prospector—the man who wandered hither and thither, killing game for a living, and spending his life in the quest for metal wealth. In all the world there could be no better material for soldiers than that afforded by these grim hunters of the mountains, these wild rough riders of the plains. They were accustomed to handling wild and savage horses; they were accustomed to following the chase with the rifle, both for sport and as a means of livelihood. Varied though their occupations had been, almost all had, at one time or another, herded cattle and hunted big game. They were hardened to life in the open, and to shifting for themselves under adverse circumstances. They were used, for all their lawless freedom, to the rough discipline of the round-up and the mining company. Some of them came from the small frontier towns; but most were from the wilderness, having left their lonely hunters' cabins and shifting cow-camps to seek new and

THE ROUGH RIDERS' CAMP IN TAMPA, FLORIDA
In Florida, the men of the Rough Riders spent their days training and their free time resting up and preparing for more training. Their rations before leaving for Cuba were of better quality and could consist of beef or pork (bacon), beans, hardtack, and coffee. Camps were kept clean and were policed frequently. While some occupied their time cleaning and maintaining their equipment, others sought recreation through pastimes such as telling tall tales, playing cards, smoking tobacco (cigarettes, cigars, pipes), and playing baseball or other sports games—or occasionally visiting a house of ill repute.

Another view of some officers wearing M1898 uniforms. One (second from left) is wearing a modified M1884 fatigue uniform. (AdeQHA)

more stirring adventures beyond the sea … There was one characteristic and distinctive contingent which could have appeared only in such a regiment as ours. From the Indian Territory there came a number of Indians—Cherokees, Chickasaws, Choctaws, and Creeks.

In its final total the unit included miners, cowboys, college students, tradesmen, writers, professors, athletes, lawmen, preachers, and clergymen. Remarkably, there were men from each of the 45 states then in existence, as well as from the four territories and from 14 countries. There were even 60 Native Americans on the roster. The integration of whites and non-whites in a single regiment was totally unheard of in the military in its day, as the United States Army remained segregated until 1948.

With regard to how the regiment received its name, Roosevelt wrote:

Wood and I were speedily commissioned as Colonel and Lieutenant-Colonel of the First United States Volunteer Cavalry. This was the official title of the regiment, but for some reason or other the public promptly christened us the "Rough Riders." At first we fought against the use of the term, but to no purpose; and when finally the Generals of Division and Brigade began to write in formal communications about our regiment as the "Rough Riders," we adopted the term ourselves.

Other names attributed to the regiment were "Teddy's Terrors," and "Wood's Weary Walkers," but it was the "Rough Riders" that stuck. The term was a familiar one in 1898; Buffalo Bill had called his famous western show "Buffalo Bill's Wild West and Congress of Rough Riders of the World."

The other "Rough Riders"

The 2nd United States Volunteer Cavalry was raised by Colonel Jay L. Torrey, and as a consequence was known as "Torrey's Rough Riders". This regiment was composed mostly of men from Wyoming. The troopers left Cheyenne on June 22, 1898 for Camp Cuba Libre, Jacksonville, Florida. At Tupelo, Mississippi, on the 26th of that month, the second section of the troop train encountered those of the first section, which resulted in the immediate death of three troopers. Three others died later, and 11 others were injured, including Colonel Torrey himself. The record of Torrey's troopers in the Florida camp shows but one "scrap," and the affair never made it beyond the confines of the company street. One of the troopers described it to the officer-of-the-day in the following manner: "It didn't amount to anything, sir. One of the boys in the Leadville troop got a little too much liquor. He came over to our troop looking for something, and he found it. I handed it to him."

These troopers of the 2nd United States Volunteer Cavalry never entered action with the Spaniards—the war ended too soon—but they at least fully proved the quality of western manhood. Indeed, the struggle made by Colonel Torrey to get his regiment into action was energetic and persistent, but futile. The regiment arrived in Jacksonville on June 28, after the fighting had begun at Santiago. An urgent appeal was made and re-made to be included in the Puerto Rican expedition, but cavalry was not needed there, and disappointment followed. The regiment remained at Camp Cuba Libre until October, when it mustered out.

The 3rd United States Volunteer Cavalry, was made up of troops from North Dakota, South Dakota, Montana, and Nebraska. The 3rd was mustered into federal service between May 12 and May 23, 1898. Commanded by Melvin Grigsby, Attorney General of South Dakota, and considered to be a "cowboy" regiment, the unit gained the name of "Grigsby's Rough Riders" after their more famous counterpart. When mustered in, the unit consisted of 45 officers and 961 men, and was organized in the following locations: troops A, B, C, D, and E—South Dakota; Troop F—Montana; troops G and H—North Dakota; troops I, L and M—Montana; Troop K—Nebraska. Troop F was organized by Will Cave of Missoula, Montana. He began organizing this embryonic troop on March 31, 1898, leading to the claim that he was the first to volunteer for service in the war.

Both the 3rd and 2nd United States Volunteer Cavalry, never saw service outside of the continental United States and appears to have spent the majority of its brief career at Camp Thomas, located on the former Civil War battlefield of Chickamauga, Georgia. The camp was one of the major United States training camps, and grew quite unhealthy as the population at the camp rose to tens of thousands of men by the late summer of 1898. With the war's fighting ending by armistice on August 13, 1898, the 3rd was no longer needed, and was mustered out at Camp Thomas on September 8 that year. During its term of service, nine men died of disease, 22 were discharged on disability, two were court-martialed, and four deserted.

TRAINING

Roosevelt noted that one of the problems at the time of raising the regiment, and subsequently, was providing material to equip the men:

> The difficulty lay in arming, equipping, mounting, and disciplining the men we selected. Hundreds of regiments were being called into existence by the National Government, and each regiment was sure to have innumerable wants to be satisfied. To a man who knew the ground as Wood did, and who was entirely aware of our national unpreparedness, it was evident that the ordnance and quartermaster's bureaus could not meet, for some time to come, one-tenth of the demands that would be made upon them; and it was all-important to get in first

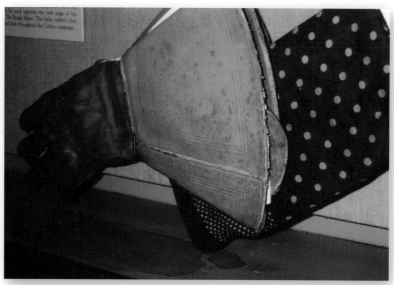

with our demands. Thanks to his knowledge of the situation and promptness, we immediately put in our requisitions for the articles indispensable for the equipment of the regiment; and then, by ceaseless worrying of excellent bureaucrats, who had no idea how to do things quickly or how to meet an emergency, we succeeded in getting our rifles, cartridges, revolvers, clothing, shelter-tents, and horse gear just in time to enable us to go on the Santiago expedition. Some of the State troops, who were already organized as National Guards, were, of course, ready, after a fashion, when the war broke out; but no other regiment which had our work to do was able to do it in anything like as quick time, and therefore no other volunteer regiment saw anything like the fighting which we did.

Training the new recruits began as soon the men were formally inducted into the regiment in San Antonio, Texas. The maintenance of proper discipline was an essential part of the process, and the men became scrupulously careful in touching their hats, and always came to attention when spoken to. Roosevelt recounted the typical routines required of the men:

Rigid guard duty was established at once, and everyone was impressed with the necessity for vigilance and watchfulness. The policing of the camp was likewise attended to with the utmost rigor. As always with new troops, they were at first indifferent to the necessity for cleanliness in camp arrangements; but on this point Colonel Wood brooked no laxity, and in a very little while the hygienic conditions of the camp were as good as those of any regular regiment. Meanwhile the men were being drilled, on foot at first, with the utmost assiduity. Every night we had officers' school, the non-commissioned officers of each troop being given similar schooling by the Captain or one of

B **MARKSMANSHIP TRAINING**
During the period of training in the United States prior to shipment to Cuba, the Rough Riders initially concentrated on cavalry tactics. However, when it was learned that they were to fight as infantry in Cuba, the emphasis shifted towards skirmish drills and other similar infantry tactics. Marksmanship was heavily concentrated on, as shown in this illustration.

Rough Riders filling their Mills cartridge belts with ammunition for their .30–.40 caliber M1896 Krag carbines. (AdeQHA)

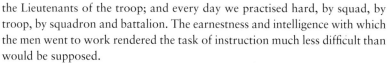

the Lieutenants of the troop; and every day we practised hard, by squad, by troop, by squadron and battalion. The earnestness and intelligence with which the men went to work rendered the task of instruction much less difficult than would be supposed.

Captain Frank Frantz of Troop A is seen wearing his M1898 uniform and M1889 campaign hat. He later became governor of the Oklahoma Territory. (AdeQHA)

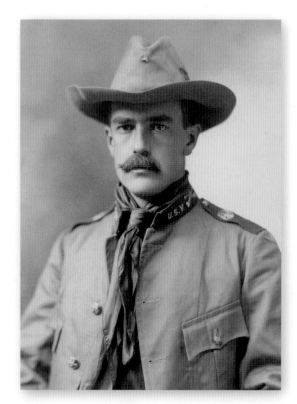

Having acquired the skill to handle the regiment in simpler forms of close and open order, on the march and in drill-ground maneuvers, the troops began to train in open order work, skirmishing and weapons firing. The regiment then moved to Tampa, Florida, where training continued and further improvements were made to drill and maneuver, both on foot and mounted. The units' tents were put up in long streets, with the officers' quarters at the upper ends of each, and the company kitchens and sinks at the opposite ends. Roosevelt noted that the sandy streets of the little town "were thronged with soldiers". The Rough Riders did not take time off from training, and, unlike the general officers and their staffs, Roosevelt rarely left camp to socialize at the Tampa Bay Hotel, built by the railroad magnate Henry B. Plant, where newspaper correspondents, foreign military attachés, and other onlookers and hangers-on gathered.

Roosevelt described the drill and training of the troops of the Rough Riders in detail:

We worked with the utmost industry, special attention being given by each troop-commander to skirmish-drill in the woods. Once or twice we had mounted drill of the regiment as a whole … Before drilling the men on horseback they had all been drilled on foot, and having gone at their work with hearty zest, they knew well the simple movements to form any kind of line or column. Wood was busy from morning till night in hurrying the final details of the equipment, and he turned the drill of the men over to me. To drill perfectly needs long practice, but to drill roughly is a thing very easy to learn indeed. We were not always right about our intervals, our lines were somewhat irregular, and our more difficult movements were executed at times in rather a haphazard way; but the essential commands and the essential movements we learned without any difficulty, and the men performed them with great dash. When we put them on horseback, there was, of course, trouble with the horses; but the horsemanship of the riders was consummate. In fact, the men were immensely interested in making their horses perform each evolution with the utmost speed and accuracy, and in forcing each unquiet, vicious brute to get into line and stay in line, whether he would or not … In short, from the very beginning the horseback drills were good fun, and everyone enjoyed them. We marched out through the adjoining country to drill wherever we found open ground, practising all the different column formations as we went. On the open ground we threw out the line to one side or the other, and in one position and the other, sometimes at the trot, sometimes at the gallop. As the men grew accustomed to the simple evolutions, we tried them more and more in skirmish drills, practising them so that they might get accustomed to advance in open order and to skirmish in any country, while the horses were held in the rear.

Much to the dismay of Colonel Roosevelt and his men, the general staff decided to leave the horses behind in Tampa because of logistical problems in transporting large number of these animals to Cuba, and to treat the cavalrymen as dismounted troops. Roosevelt always regretted this. He felt that the horse was the most important weapon with which to strike the first blow against the enemy.

The newly formed 1st United States Volunteer Cavalry gradually began to take shape after nearly a month of training, with observers remarking on the improvements made by the men. Both officers and men applied themselves to their drill tasks. Roosevelt noted:

The life of a Rough Rider before embarking for Cuba was filled with training, marching, and other chores that their NCOs and officers deemed necessary in order to keep the men occupied. (AdeQHA)

Horsemanship and cavalry tactics were taught at first, but they were replaced with infantry tactics when the regiment found out that their mounts were not coming with them to Cuba. Captain Woodbury Kane and William Tiffany, holding a guidon, are seen posing with fellow Rough Riders of Troop K. (AdeQHA)

The officers speedily grew to realize that they must not be over-familiar with their men, and yet that they must care for them in every way. The men, in return, began to acquire those habits of attention to soldierly detail which mean so much in making a regiment. Above all, every man felt, and had constantly instilled into him, a keen pride of the regiment, and a resolute purpose to do his whole duty uncomplainingly, and, above all, to win glory by the way he handled himself in battle.

APPEARANCE

Owing to a lack of khaki material at the onset of the war, the enlisted men were issued with the Model 1884 Fatigue Uniform of brown cotton duck material, which was originally intended for fatigue duty. The intent was for the canvas uniform to be worn while manual labor was conducted, thereby saving the more expensive wool service uniform from wear and tear. Given the lack of available khaki officer's coats, officers of the regiment even purchased these fatigue uniforms and had them altered with standing collars, colored cuffs, and/or officers' shoulder straps—depending on the personal tastes of the officer. The officers' uniform comprised the dark blue Model 1895 Undress Uniform. It was the officers' version of the "sack coat" and the uniform was laced with black mohair. Regulations required that shoulder straps and gilt collar devices be worn on the coat. A white or summer version of the coat was also issued, however no rank or other devices were worn until 1901. The army regulation prescribed that the undress uniform for officers was to be used for "marches, squad and company drills, other drills when authorized by the Commanding Officer, and for fatigue duty and ordinary wear" (Jacobsen 1899). However, some period photographs have shown officers wearing enlisted men's five-buttoned sack coats with shoulder straps on the battlefield. This may be in fact the old Model (hereafter, M) 1885 blouse that was identical to the enlisted men's, but which was constructed of much finer quality materials. The standard trousers were the same as the enlisted men's, with the correct one-and-a-half-inch stripes colored with the facings of the wearer's respective branch of arms. The Model 1895 Undress Uniform was also adopted by West Point and other military

Men of Troop H riding into Tampa. This troop remained in Tampa to care for the horses while the rest of the regiment left for Cuba. (AdeQHA)

schools, with its color being the traditional cadet grey, and is still in use by West Point cadets at the time of writing. The uniform was worn with the Model 1895 Officer's Cap or the M1889 Campaign Hat that was worn by all ranks.

The insignia worn on the officers' undress coats consisted of the letters "U.S." or "U.S.V." in gothic design embroidered in either gold or gilt metal. For the Corps of Engineers, the insignia was embroidered in silver, or made of silver, and was worn on each side of the collar about 5/8 inch from the letters "U. S." or "U. S. V." The following distinctive insignia was prescribed in the 1899 Uniform Regulations for use by officers within the cavalry: two crossed sabers, one inch high, with the number of the regiment above the intersection, and made of gold or gilt metal, or embroidered in gold. Insignia worn on the new khaki uniforms were mostly of gilt metal and were meant to be removable.

Those members of the Rough Riders recruited from the regular army or state troops reporting for duty were mostly uniformed and equipped like regular army troops. For field use the M1883 Blouse, M1895 Forage Cap, and M1889 Campaign Hat were utilized, as well as the M1884 Dress Coat and M1881 Dress Helmet for formal occasions. Officers wore uniforms similar to those worn by their regular counterparts. All branches wore light blue kersey trousers (with the cavalry having reinforced seats and legs), with a colored stripe (denoting branch) down the length of each side of the trousers. In terms of footwear, a pair of brown cotton duck leggings were to be worn over russet leather shoes.

The soldiers and even their officers preferred to wear the M1883 Army Overshirt, usually referred to as the "campaign shirt." This shirt was widely worn as unofficial campaign uniform by most soldiers in the Spanish-American War. By 1901, the overshirt had become regulation drill and campaign uniform for "extremely warm weather." This was to be used as an alternative to the heavier, five-button blouse and was practical and comfortable in harsh tropical climates. The shirts were of blue flannel and had two large breast pockets.

The experimental Tan Duck Uniform of 1898 had many variations and was issued to various regular units and some state troops. The colors on the stand-up collar and cuffs (and occasionally on the pocket flaps) denoted branch of service. The M1898 Tan Duck Uniform closely resembled the M1888 Summer Sack Coat, but featured the addition of pockets. The epaulets denoted branch of service by color (with yellow for the cavalry). The later M1899 Field Blouse was the final version of the cotton uniform used in the United States' occupation of Cuba and the Phillipine insurrection. Initially there wasn't enough material to fulfil the demands of the army, and so the bulk of those used early in the war were purchased by officers and NCOs. Theodore Roosevelt procured his custom-tailored uniform from Brooks Brothers Clothiers of New York. It was not until after the Battle of San Juan Hill that the rank and file were issued the new khaki uniforms, with yellow cuffs, collars and shoulder straps.

For enlisted men, rank was displayed on both sleeves of their uniforms and overcoats on M1872 cloth chevrons. These were worn points down, and were located above the elbow on the dress coat and fatigue blouse, while those on the overcoat were worn below the elbow. The bars of the chevrons were separated by black silk chain stitching. Chevrons for the khaki field uniforms were as previously described, "but of such material as may be found most suitable for service." Specialty ratings were also utilized on an enlisted man's sleeves, and if the wearer was an NCO they would be worn within the bars as a central piece of the chevron. These comprised: cook—a cook's cap of cloth conforming in color to arm of service, except Signal Corps, which would be black upon white cloth; farrier—a horseshoe of cloth 4.5 inches long and 3.75 inches wide, worn toe uppermost; saddler—a saddler's round knife, of cloth; and mechanic and artificer—two crossed hammers, of cloth.

Enlisted rank was indicated in the following manner: regimental sergeant major—three bars and an arc of three bars; regimental quartermaster sergeant—three bars and a tie of three bars; regimental commissary sergeant—three bars and a tie of three bars, having a crescent (points front) 0.75 inches above the inner angle of chevron; squadron or battalion sergeant majors—three bars and an arc of two bars; chief musician—three bars and an arc of two bars, with a bugle pattern worn on caps in the center; chief trumpeter—three bars and an arc of one bar, with a bugle pattern worn on caps in the center; principal musician—three bars and a bugle; drum major—three bars and two embroidered crossed batons; ordnance sergeant—three bars and a star; post quartermaster sergeant—three bars and a crossed key and pen; post commissary sergeant—three bars and a crescent (points to the front) 1.25 inches above the inner angle of chevron; hospital steward—three bars and an arc of one bar, of emerald green cloth, enclosing a red cross (a green cross with white borders after 1899); acting hospital steward—the same as for a hospital steward, omitting the arc; first sergeant—three bars and a lozenge; troop, battery, or company quartermaster sergeant—three bars and a tie of one bar; sergeant—three bars; regimental and battalion color sergeant—three bars and a sphere, 1.25 inches in diameter; corporal—two bars; lance corporal—one bar. The 1899 Uniform Regulations specified that "a lance corporal shall wear, in addition to the uniform of a private, a chevron having one bar of lace or braid; holding a renewed appointment, he shall wear the uniform of a corporal, except the chevron shall have but one bar of lace or braid."

WEAPONS AND EQUIPMENT

One of the most important personal weapons issued to the Rough Riders was the revolver. The main model used was the M1872 Colt single action Army revolver. This 45-caliber handgun was refurbished and had its 7.5-inch barrel replaced with a 5.5-inch barrel by military armorers in the 1890s. The shortened Colt revolvers were known as the "Artillery models." Hundreds of surplus Colts were purchased by various state militias, including the 1st United States Volunteer Cavalry, at the onset of the Spanish-American War.

Rough Riders walking their mounts back to camp. Note the large amount of equipment carried by the men and their horses. (AdeQHA)

Regular troops and officers were issued the new Colt Army and Navy Revolvers (models 1892, 1894, 1895, 1896, 1901, and 1903—the differences between these models are mostly minor). Well over 290,000 Colt 38-caliber revolvers were made. A few Remington M1890 single-action Army revolvers were recorded as being used during the Spanish-American War; these were manufactured between 1891 and 1894, and some 2,000 examples were produced. The M1890 revolver closely resembles the M1872 Colt single action Army revolver, but its caliber was .44–.40 and so was never officially adopted by the military. The M1872 Colt single action Army revolver and double-action revolvers were issued alongside the M1897 holster in russet leather.

Theodore Roosevelt carried a unique Colt Model 1895 Army and Navy Revolver. On February 15, 1898, the battleship USS *Maine* exploded in Havana Harbor, killing 266 sailors and Marines. A salvage crew led by Roosevelt's brother-in-law, William Cowles, recovered a double-action revolver from the wreckage, which Cowles later gave to Roosevelt. Six months later, as the Rough Riders stormed San Juan Hill in Cuba, Roosevelt carried the same revolver as a memorial to the men whose lives were lost on the USS *Maine*. The engravings on the gun's frame read "From the sunken battleship *Maine*" on one side, and "July 1st 1898, San Juan, carried and used by Col. Theodore Roosevelt" on the other.

Interestingly, no training was undertaken for use of the traditional cavalry weapon of the saber. With regard to the choice of revolver over the saber, Roosevelt noted in his memoirs:

> Many of my cavalry friends in the past had insisted to me that the revolver was a better weapon than the sword—among them Basil Duke, the noted Confederate cavalry leader, and Captain Frank Edwards, whom I had met when elk-hunting on the head-waters of the Yellowstone and the Snake. Personally, I knew too little to decide as to the comparative merits of the two arms; but I did know that it was a great deal better to use the arm with which our men were already proficient. They were therefore armed with what might be called their natural weapon, the revolver.

With regard to shoulder weapons, the Rough Riders were chiefly armed with the regular US Army cavalry carbine, the Norwegian-designed Krag-Jorgensen repeating bolt-action rifle, Winchester rifles, and "Trapdoor" Springfield rifles. At the time of the outbreak of the Spanish-American War, the majority of regular US Army troops were issued with the .30–.40 Krag-Jorgensen repeating bolt-action rifle (commonly known as the "Krag") and carbine (models 1892, 1894, 1896, 1898, and 1899). However, the bulk of state troops had not yet been issued these new firearms and were therefore still using the obsolete .45–.70 "Trapdoor" Springfield rifle and carbine

C **TROOPER, 1ST UNITED STATES VOLUNTEER CAVALRY**
This trooper of the 1st United States Volunteer Cavalry during the Cuban campaign wears the M1884 fatigue uniform in its distinctive brown color (**1**) and the M1889 campaign hat (**2**). His equipment consists of the Mills M1896 cavalry cartridge belt (**3**), M1881 holster for his Colt artillery model revolver (**4**), M1878 haversack (**5**), M1885/1898 canteen (**6**), rolled blanket (**7**), leggings (**8**), and the M1893 campaign shoes (**9**). He is armed with the M1896 Krag carbine (**10**) that is protected with a canvas breech cover (**11**). His haversack would contain his eating utensils, food (such as hardtack, **12**), M1874 mess kit, and personal items. A tin cup would have been attached to his haversack (**13**). Also shown is the cavalry crossed swords cap badge (**14**).

C

3

14

6

2

4

7

5

11

1

12

13

10

8

9

ABOVE LEFT
A very well maintained camp street of the 1st United States Volunteer Cavalry. Note the regiment's horses in the distance. (AdeQHA)

ABOVE RIGHT
An excellent study of horse equipment used by the Rough Riders. Note the Krag carbine with breech cover slipped into its holster. (AdeQHA)

(models 1870, 1873, 1877, 1884, and 1888). As the Rough Riders were newly raised and lacked the proper connections, it is more than likely that many troopers were issued with this type of obsolescent weapon in its carbine form. The "Trapdoor" Springfields used black powder cartridges, which, when discharged, would reveal the firer's position to enemy snipers and artillerymen. In the context of the Spanish-American War, the latter would be armed with Mauser bolt-action rifles, which fired smokeless powder ammunition, giving them a distinct advantage. Roosevelt recounted his commanding officer's reaction to this state of affairs:

> Wood thoroughly realized what the Ordnance Department failed to realize, namely, the inestimable advantage of smokeless powder; and, moreover, he was bent upon our having the weapons of the regulars, for this meant that we would be brigaded with them, and it was evident that they would do the bulk of the fighting if the war were short. Accordingly, by acting with the utmost vigor and promptness, he succeeded in getting our regiment armed with the Krag-Jorgensen carbine used by the regular cavalry.

The Krag-Jorgensen was based upon the rifles used in Denmark and fired a smokeless powder cartridge, a first for United States firearms. The Krags were bolt-action operated, .30–.40-caliber centerfire rifles, and were manufactured at the Springfield Armory in Massachusetts, the US military's primary small-arms manufacturing site. Each Krag magazine held five rounds of ammunition, and was loaded from the right side through a large, hinged loading gate. Blade-type front sights set in a high stud near the muzzle appeared on all models.

Some of the source materials from this period make reference to Winchester M1895 lever-action carbines that were chambered to take the .30-caliber Krag-Jorgensen round; these were carried by some of the officers, including Colonel Roosevelt. The latter recalls one incident of note regarding the Winchesters, the regiment's return from Cuba:

> Bob Wren … had joined us very late and we could not get him a Krag carbine; so I had given him my Winchester, which carried the government cartridge; and when he was mustered out he carried it home in triumph, to the envy of his fellows, who themselves had to surrender their beloved rifles.

In addition, Roosevelt noted, the Rough Riders acquired a limited number of crew-served weapons, comprising "two rapid-fire Colt automatic guns, the gift of Stevens, Kane, Tiffany, and one or two others of the New York men, and also a dynamite gun, under the immediate charge of Sergeant Borrowe."

Given that the Rough Riders fought dismounted during the Cuban expedition, the men ended up carrying many more items of equipment than they had expected to at the outset. In a letter to his father dated June 28, 1898, Private Kirk McCurdy wrote:

> Those marches were pretty tough and lots of strong men gave out. Our load was pretty heavy. We carry our pajamas, underclothes and other articles rolled in a heavy blanket which is rolled in a half tent and covered by a rubber blanket; this goes over our shoulders. We have a carbine, one hundred rounds of ammunition in a belt, a canteen, a haversack with three days' rations (generally), and axe, pick or shovel, which is pretty good load to carry four or five miles in the hot sun. [McCurdy 1902]

In addition, some Rough Riders were issued with Collins Model 22 and similar model machetes. A regimental adjutant of the Rough Riders remarked:

> None of the troops were supplied with machetes as had been originally intended. Later the detail assigned to the Colt rapid fire guns was armed with them. [Stewart 1998, p. 53]

CONDITIONS OF SERVICE

Pay
The pay staff of the US Army at the turn of the 20th century included a Paymaster General, two Assistant Paymasters General with the rank of colonel, three Deputy Paymasters General with the rank of lieutenant colonel, and 20 Paymasters with the rank of major. For the volunteer army, to which the

The Rough Riders in full kit and marching order. All are wearing the M1884 fatigue uniform. (AdeQHA)

Theodore Roosevelt becomes acclimatized to the temperate climate of Tampa, Florida. (AdeQHA)

Rough Riders belonged, this staff was increased by the creation of an additional Paymaster for every two regiments. Under the war conditions of 1898, the men of the volunteer army were paid by the Paymasters directly. The right of a soldier to receive pay from the US Government was first established by his commission, if he was an officer, and by the appearance of his name on the muster roll, if he was an enlisted man. When a man was paid off the first time, he signed the payroll in receipt, which established his right to another month's pay if he was not killed before the month expired. In the event that he was killed in action, the matter passed out of the hands of the Pay Department and was referred to the Auditor for the War Department, who determined what proportion of the soldier's wages for that month was earned before his death. In the words of a report entitled "Paying Men in Service," which appeared in *The New York Times* of July 3, 1898, "The Government is generous with pensions, but strict in its accounts with the men who die in its service."

Army pay was supposed to be received at the end of every month. However, the amount of time involved in making up and forwarding the payrolls from troops fighting in Cuba, Puerto Rico, and the Philippines meant that the Pay Department could only pay the men once every two months. The report "Paying Men in Service" provides an idea of the scale of the task in hand:

> General Shafter's entire army of some 15,000 men was paid up to the last day of May before they sailed from Tampa, and all the troops at San Francisco bound for the Philippines have been given two months' pay, one month in advance ... For the troops now operating in Cuba to be paid off every two months, something like $1,500,000 will be required. This money, in gold and silver coin, will be shipped in the transport or supply ships of the War Department plying between Tampa and Cuba, escorted by a force of Paymasters, who will distribute it to the men in the field. A two-months' payment will be due the men in Gen. Shafter's command on July 31, by which time they may be in Puerto Rico.

The pay of privates in the United States volunteer and regular armies during the Spanish-American War was $15.60 a month – representing an increase of 20 percent on the peacetime pay of $13 a month. In a diary entry dated August 7, 1898, nearly a month after the Battle of San Juan Hill, Private Fitch of the 1st United States Volunteer Cavalry wrote:

> We went aboard the "Miami," a fairly good transport, soon after arriving. Then I walked about town & bought a few trifles but was called back to the boat by the report that the "paymaster was aboard." After waiting some time our troop was given 2 months pay—$31.20—for time from June 1 to Aug. 1. [Fitch 1997, p. 198]

Feeding the regiment

Because of the rapid move toward war with Spain the United States military was caught unprepared, and had failed to stockpile food in order to adequately feed the thousands of new troops coming into the ranks. It took a while for the supplies and distribution to be organized into a manageable system. There were times when the regimental officers would pay out of their pockets so that their men could be fed, as Roosevelt did while his men were en route to Tampa, supplying the men with buckets of hot coffee two or three times a day. However, it was only when the men arrived in Tampa that it became clear just how overwhelmed the army was with regard to the logistical challenges it was facing, as Roosevelt made clear in his memoirs:

Camp life consisted of resting from the heavy chores as well as playing games, sharing stories, and drinking. The mess tent in the distance is filled with crates of hardtack, the daily staple of a Spanish-American War soldier. (AdeQHA)

> It was four days later that we disembarked, in a perfect welter of confusion. Tampa lay in the pine-covered sand-flats at the end of a one-track railroad, and everything connected with both military and railroad matters was in an almost inextricable tangle. There was no one to meet us or to tell us where we were to camp, and no one to issue us food for the first twenty-four hours; while the railroad people unloaded us wherever they pleased, or rather wherever the jam of all kinds of trains rendered it possible. We had to buy the men food out of our own pockets, and to seize wagons in order to get our spare baggage taken to the camping ground which we at last found had been allotted to us.

The standard field rations for a soldier had changed little since the War Between the States (1861–65, also known as the Civil War), and was based around the central components of hardtack (also known as "ship's biscuit" and "sea bread"), bacon, and coffee beans. Hardtack took the form of a large, hard biscuit and was made with an unsalted, unleavened, flour-and-water dough. After it was baked, it was dried to lengthen its shelf life. By Congressional acts in 1860 and 1861 the variety of the ration was increased noticeably. Besides the coffee and sugar components, which had been added in the 1830s, the flour component was increased to 22 ounces, and at the same time potatoes, yeast powder, and pepper were incorporated into the rations, increasing the components from 9 to 12 items as follows: 20 ounces of beef, 2.4 ounces of sugar, 22 ounces of flour .32 of a gill of vinegar, 7 ounces of potatoes, .64 ounces of salt, .045 ounces of yeast, .04 ounces of pepper, 2.65 ounces of dried beans, and 1.6 ounces of green coffee. Soldiers were also issued .64 ounces of soap and .24 ounces of candles. Very few changes were made to the ration allowance between the Civil War and the Spanish-American War. The potato ration was increased, and the yeast component was replaced with baking powder; also, the flour component reverted back to the 18 oz. allowance used in the Mexican War of 1846–48, and the issue of dried beans was decreased. The nutritional value of this ration varied only slightly with that of the Civil War period.

Private Roger S. Fitch of the 1st United States Volunteer Cavalry recounted the following conditions in his diary entry dated June 17, 1898, while awaiting the departure of the invasion fleet from Port Tampa for Cuba:

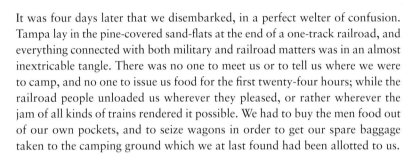

We have been living on hard-tack, coffee, & salt-horse since the 7th & it's getting slightly monotonous. Almost impossible to buy anything aboard—even at outrageous prices. Sandwiches can occasionally be bought for 25 cents each, lemons at 10 cents each, onions—3 for 25 cents, beer 30 cents a pint, & some boys got some poor whiskey at $4.00 … (later, as high as $10.00 for a quart was offered & refused). [Fitch 1997, 195]

During the Spanish-American War the prescribed rations comprised beef (or its equivalent), flour or bread, baking powder, beans, (fresh) potatoes, green coffee, sugar, vinegar, salt, pepper, soap, and candles. Private Fitch noted his meals in several entries especially with one entry, dated 29 June, reading:

Have had nothing but bacon, coffee & hard-tack for several days—& 1/2 rations at that! Hard tack are musty & so we fry them in grease to make them palatable. [Fitch 1997, p. 196]

Progress in the preparation, handling, shipping, and storage of foods was considered to be sufficiently advanced by this stage to justify the procurement of large supplies of fresh and canned meats. However, the spoilage of great quantities of those items, with the resultant deleterious effects on the health of the soldier, remains a controversial blot on the military subsistence record of this era. The lack of and spoilage of fresh foods certainly did contribute to the mortality statistics, which show that 14 soldiers died from illness and disease for every one who died from the direct effects of battle. An example of the poor quality of the canned rations that were sometimes supplied is given by Roosevelt in his memoirs. While the Rough Riders were aboard the transports waiting to sail for Cuba, Roosevelt commented:

The travel rations which had been issued to the men for the voyage were not sufficient, because the meat was very bad indeed; and when a ration consists of only four or five items, which taken together just meet the requirements of a strong and healthy man, the loss of one item is a serious thing. If we had been given canned corned beef we would have been all right, but instead of this the soldiers were issued horrible stuff called "canned fresh beef." There was no salt in it. At the best it was stringy and tasteless; at the worst it was nauseating. Not one-fourth of it was ever eaten at all, even when the men became very hungry. There were no facilities for the men to cook anything. There was no ice for them; the water was not good; and they had no fresh meat or fresh vegetables.

While in Cuba, the logistics involved in supplying the troops with food, ammunition, and other supplies plagued the commissary and quartermaster departments, as Roosevelt made clear:

> There was nothing like enough transportation with the army, whether in the way of wagons or mule-trains; exactly as there had been no sufficient number of landing-boats with the transports. The officers' baggage had come up, but none of us had much, and the shelter-tents proved only a partial protection against the terrific downpours of rain. These occurred almost every afternoon, and turned the camp into a tarn, and the trails into torrents and quagmires. We were not given quite the proper amount of food, and what we did get, like most of the clothing issued us, was fitter for the Klondyke than for Cuba. We got enough salt pork and hardtack for the men, but not the full ration of coffee and sugar, and nothing else. I organized a couple of expeditions back to the seacoast, taking the strongest and best walkers and also some of the officers' horses and a stray mule or two, and brought back beans and canned tomatoes. These I got partly by great exertions on my part, and partly by the aid of Colonel Weston of the Commissary Department, a particularly energetic man whose services were of great value. A silly regulation forbade my purchasing canned vegetables, etc., except for the officers; and I had no little difficulty in getting round this regulation, and purchasing (with my own money, of course) what I needed for the men.

While campaigning in Cuba, the men were from time to time able to supplement their meager rations by acquiring captured Spanish rations (rice, black beans, tocino, garbanzo beans, and flour) or by bartering with the local

The field kitchen of the Rough Riders while in Tampa. (AdeQHA)

Cuban populace. Things did improve in the course of time. Private Roger S. Fitch of the 1st United States Volunteer Cavalry was taken ill by "the fever" at the Battle of San Juan Hill. He spent six days in hospital, and, upon his return to camp, he wrote in his diary of the changes to and increase in the men's rations:

> Getting better though still pretty weak. Great appetite. Lost about 15 lbs. during my attack of the fever. Are having flour, baking-powder, some cornmeal, rice, etc. issued, a very agreeable change from bacon & hard-tack "straight." [Fitch 1997, p. 197]

He excitedly further added a few days later:

> Had fresh beef to-day for the first time in 6 or 7 weeks! Had fried tenderloin steaks for dinner, & soup & stew for supper—"out of sight." [p. 198]

Recreation and pastimes

As in all armies, the men of the Rough Riders found several means of passing the time or putting their minds at ease. Most played cards, gambled, smoked tobacco pipes or cigars, played pranks on each other, or talked. While the men were en route to Cuba, Roosevelt noted:

The 1st United States Volunteer Cavalry had three regimental mascots: a mountain lion, an eagle, and a dog. One of the Rough Riders is wearing a medal presented to him by Roosevelt upon the regiment's return to the United States. (AdeQHA)

The men on the ship were young and strong, eager to face what lay hidden before them, eager for adventure where risk was the price of gain. Sometimes they talked of what they might do in the future, and wondered whether we were to attack Santiago or Puerto Rico. At other times, as they lounged in groups, they told stories of their past— stories of the mining camps and the cattle ranges, of hunting bear and deer, of war-trails against the Indians, of lawless deeds of violence and the lawful violence by which they were avenged, of brawls in saloons, of shrewd deals in cattle and sheep, of successful quest for the precious metals; stories of brutal wrong and brutal appetite, melancholy love-tales, and memories of nameless heroes—masters of men and tamers of horses.

Of all the forms of recreation that the men took part in, the drinking of alcohol was the one that most of them shared. There are numerous accounts of their passion for liquor in the letters and diaries of the individual Rough Riders themselves, as well as in Roosevelt's memoirs. Following the end of the war and upon returning to the United States, a situation developed that required Roosevelt to take control immediately:

Soon after leaving port the captain of the ship notified me that his stokers and engineers were insubordinate and drunken, due, he thought, to liquor which my men had given them. I at once started a search of the ship, explaining to the men that they could not keep the liquor; that if they surrendered whatever

Chaplain Henry Brown giving religious service in Cuba. (AdeQHA)

they had to me I should return it to them when we went ashore; and that meanwhile I would allow the sick to drink when they really needed it; but that if they did not give the liquor to me of their own accord I would throw it overboard. About seventy flasks and bottles were handed to me, and I found and threw overboard about twenty. This at once put a stop to all drunkenness. The stokers and engineers were sullen and half mutinous, so I sent a detail of my men down to watch them and see that they did their work under the orders of the chief engineer; and we reduced them to obedience in short order.

Music was one element that tightened the camaraderie within the Rough Riders. The song *There'll Be a Hot Time in the Old Town Tonight* was a great favorite during the Spanish-American War of 1898, although it had actually been written 12 years earlier by Theodore Metz, bandleader of The McIntyre and Heath Minstrels. Metz was inspired to write it when he saw a group of black children putting out a fire in Old Town, Louisiana. The Mcintyre and Heath Minstrels used it as a marching tune for its street parades, but interest in the song caught on when Joe Hayden wrote words to accompany the music, leading to Teddy Roosevelt's Rough Riders adopting it as their personal anthem in Cuba:

Come along, get you ready
Wear your bran', bran' new gown
For there's gwine to be a meeting
In that good, good old town
Where you knowded everybody
And they all know-ded you
And you've got a rabbit's foot
To keep away de hoo-doo.
When you hear that the preaching does begin
Bend down low for to drive away your sin
And when you gets religion, you want to shout and sing
There'll be a hot time in the old town tonight, my baby

[Chorus]

When you hear dem a bells go ding ling ling
All join round and sweetly you must sing
And when the verse am through in the chorus all join in
There'll be a hot time in the old town tonight.

There'll be girls for ev'ry body
In that good, good old town,
For there's Miss Consola Davis
And there's Miss Gondolia Brown
And there's Miss Johanna Beasly
She am dressed all in red,
I just hugged her and I kissed her
And to me then she said:
"Please oh please, oh do not let me fall,
You're all mine and I love you best of all,
And you must be my man, or I'll have no man at all,
There'll be a hot time in the old town tonight, my baby."

Trooper William Pollock was one of the few Native Americans to enlist with the Rough Riders, adding to the wide diversity that made the regiment unique in comparison with other United States military formations of the day. (AdeQHA)

The Rough Riders cultivated a grudging respect for their Spanish foes, and held them in higher esteem than the Cubans that they came to "liberate." (AdeQHA

Discipline

Discipline was of extreme importance and closely monitored among the men of the Rough Riders. Most of the men were diligent and carried out their duties with care and dedication. However, because of the "Wild West" tendencies and rough characters of some of the men who filled the ranks, lapses did occur. Whilst stationed in San Antonia one of the Rough Riders decided to "paint the town red," and was put into jail by the city authorities, resulting in his being left behind when the men of his unit left the area. Other misdemeanors were dealt with by the officers of the Rough Riders themselves, and due care was taken to make sure that any offences did not reoccur. However, the officers understood human nature, especially once the men had been through extreme circumstances of combat, and they tended to overlook any minor offences committed by those who had served admirably under fire. Many instances were put down to overexuberance, and were excused, being considered a natural means for the men to release any pressure that had built up during the Cuban campaign. Such tolerance and flexibility were demonstrated in a very clear manner when the regiment returned home at the end of the war, as Roosevelt recalled:

> I had assumed a large authority in giving rewards and punishments. In particular I had looked on court-martials much as Peter Bell looked on primroses—they were court-martials and nothing more, whether resting on the authority of a lieutenant-colonel or of a major-general. The mustering-out officer, a thorough soldier, found to his horror that I had used the widest discretion both in imposing heavy sentences which I had no power to impose on men who shirked their duties, and, where men atoned for misconduct by marked gallantry, in blandly remitting sentences approved by my chief of division. However, I had done substantial, even though somewhat rude and irregular, justice—and no harm could result, as we were just about to be mustered out.

BELIEF AND BELONGING

What made the officers and men of the Rough Riders willing to take on a fight on foreign soil? What made them soldiers? Colonel Theodore Roosevelt tried to explain their motivation in his memoirs *The Rough Riders*:

> Everyone seemed to realize that he had undertaken most serious work. They all earnestly wished for a chance to distinguish themselves, and fully appreciated that they ran the risk not merely of death, but of what was infinitely worse—namely, failure at the crisis to perform duty well; and they strove earnestly so to train themselves, and the men under them, as to minimize the possibility of such disgrace. Every officer and every man was taught continually to look forward to the day of battle eagerly, but with an entire sense of the drain that would then be made upon his endurance and resolution. They were also taught that, before the battle came, the rigorous performance of the countless irksome duties of the camp and the march was demanded from all alike, and that no excuse would be tolerated for failure to perform duty. Very few of the men had gone into the regiment lightly, and the fact that they did their duty so well may be largely attributed to the seriousness with which these eager, adventurous young fellows approached their work.

Like many military men, the troopers of the Rough Riders bonded with each other through the use of nicknames. These fostered camaraderie among fellow soldiers and created a sense of their being a part of the regiment. Nicknames were even conferred on the men's superiors. Roosevelt recalled some of the names that were meted out, and the droll humour attached to each one:

> A brave but fastidious member of a well-known Eastern club, who was serving in the ranks, was christened "Tough Ike"; and his bunkie, the man who shared his shelter-tent, who was a decidedly rough cow-puncher, gradually acquired the name of "The Dude." One unlucky and simple-minded cow-puncher, who

ABOVE
Many accounts written by members of the Rough Riders indicated precious little respect and praise for the Cuban Army of Liberation, despite the fact that these men had cleared the beaches for the American landings to occur and had been waging their third war of independence since 1895. (AdeQHA)

BELOW LEFT
Rough Riders offloading from their transport, *Yucatan*, and heading toward the beaches. (AdeQHA)

BELOW RIGHT
The Rough Riders landing at Daiquirí, Cuba. (AdeQHA)

had never been east of the great plains in his life, unwarily boasted that he had an aunt in New York, and ever afterward went by the name of "Metropolitan Bill." A huge red-headed Irishman was named "sheeny Solomon." A young Jew who developed into one of the best fighters in the regiment accepted, with entire equanimity, the name of "Pork-chop." We had quite a number of professional gamblers, who, I am bound to say, usually made good soldiers. One, who was almost abnormally quiet and gentle, was called "Hell Roarer"; while another, who in point of language and deportment was his exact antithesis, was christened "Prayerful James."

Support for the Cuban cause

The Spanish-American War was a direct result of the Cuban struggle for independence from Spanish rule. Since the early years of the 19th century, many Americans had watched with sympathy the series of revolutions that ended Spanish authority throughout South America, Central America, and Mexico. Many people in the United States were irritated that the Spanish flag continued to fly in Cuba and Puerto Rico. The brutality with which Spain put down Cuban demands for a degree of local autonomy and personal liberty aroused both sympathy and anger. Support for the cause of Cuban independence had deep historical roots in the United States, and this cause became the stated objective of the war—and the one to which the men of the Rough Riders adhered when they volunteered for service in Cuba.

The Cubans revolted in 1895 under the inspired leadership of Cuban patriot Jose Martí. The revolt was prompted by the failure of the Spanish Government to institute reforms it had promised the Cuban people at the conclusion of a rebellion against Spanish rule known as the Ten Years' War (1868–78). To put down the 1895 rebellion, the Spanish Government poured more than 100,000 troops into the island. General Valeriano Weyler y Nicolau, known as the "Butcher" for his ruthless suppression of earlier revolts, was sent to the island as captain general and military governor. He immediately rounded up the peasant population and put them in concentration camps in or near garrison towns. Thousands died of starvation and disease.

The brutality of "Butcher" Weyler aroused great indignation in the United States. The general anger was exploited by sensational press reports, which exaggerated Weyler's ruthlessness. In 1897 the Spanish Government became alarmed at the belligerent tone of public opinion in the United States. Weyler was recalled, and overtures were made to the rebels. The latter rejected an offer of autonomy, however, and were determined to fight for complete independence. After the Spanish-American War, Cuba received its "independence" from the United States, although this had been granted under the conditions of the Platt Amendment, which, among other things, gave the United States the unconditional right to intervene in Cuba's internal affairs, and perpetual rights to the coaling station at Guantanamo Bay. By 1902, the Cubans had been forced to accept the Platt Amendment as the only alternative to remaining under direct United States military rule. A cycle of dependence on United States approval had begun, which would only eventually be broken by Fidel Castro's revolution against the military dictator General Fulgencio Batista y Zaldívar in 1959. In contrast, while Cuba became a nation, the newly acquired territories of Guam, the Philippines, and Puerto Rico became American possessions.

Sergeant Nevin P. Guitilias of Troop H in full campaign kit. He had been chosen to be part of the crew of the dynamite gun that accompanied the regiment. (AdeQHA)

Roosevelt's own motivations for fighting in Cuba can be clearly seen in the opening pages of his memoirs:

> While my party was in opposition, I had preached, with all the fervor and zeal I possessed, our duty to intervene in Cuba, and to take this opportunity of driving the Spaniard from the Western World. Now that my party had come to power, I felt it incumbent on me, by word and deed, to do all I could to secure the carrying out of the policy in which I so heartily believed; and from the beginning I had determined that, if a war came, somehow or other, I was going to the front.

Manifest destiny and the rise of American imperialism

An important factor in the United States' decision to go to war was its growing imperialistic tendencies, as seen in the mounting efforts to extend American influence overseas. The increasingly aggressive behavior of the United States was often justified by references to its "manifest destiny"—a belief that territorial expansion by the United States was both inevitable and divinely ordained. This belief enjoyed widespread support among United States citizens and politicians in the 19th century.

"Manifest destiny" was promoted by the publishers of several prominent United States newspapers, particularly William Randolph Hearst, the publisher of The *New York Journal*, and Joseph Pulitzer, the publisher of the *New York World*. Their newspapers printed a steady stream of sensational stories about alleged atrocities committed by the Spanish in Cuba, calling for the United States to intervene on the side of the Cubans. The spirit of imperialism growing in the United States—fuelled by supporters of "manifest destiny"—led many Americans to believe that the United States needed to take aggressive steps, both economically and militarily, to establish itself as a true world power.

Roosevelt and his Rough Riders used a Sims-Dudley gun during the siege of Santiago, with mixed results. The gun did work as intended, but it was mechanically unreliable and not very accurate. On balance Roosevelt was unenthusiastic, but found it "more effective than the regular artillery." (AdeQHA)

A far cry from the clean company streets and tents in a row as in Tampa. These shelters actually covered bombproofs built as a means of protection from Spanish artillery. (AdeQHA)

Rough Riders became accustomed to trench warfare during the siege of Santiago de Cuba. (AdeQHA)

Another facet of manifest destiny was the Monroe doctrine—a principle of United States policy originated by President James Monroe during his time in office (1817–25). The Monroe doctrine held that any intervention by external powers in the politics of the Americas was a potentially hostile act against the United States. The principle arose partly from a conflict with Russia over ownership of the northwest coast of North America, and partly from the fear that reactionary European states would attempt to take over the Latin American countries that had become independent from Spain. President McKinley invoked the Monroe doctrine against Spain, and demanded that the colonial power grant Cuba independence. Naturally Spain refused, and war ensued.

The reunification of a divided nation

The Spanish-American War was the common denominator that finally brought unity to the United States in the wake of a devastating civil war, a conflict that had all but divided the country for over three decades. As the Rough Riders were being transported by rail from San Antonio, Texas to Tampa, Florida, Colonel Roosevelt reflected on the powerful influence this conflict had over the men of his unit, and the strongly unifying effect the war would have on the nation as a whole:

> We were traveling through a region where practically all the older men had served in the Confederate Army, and where the younger men had all their lives long drunk in the endless tales told by their elders, at home, and at the cross-roads taverns, and in the court-house squares, about the cavalry of Forrest and Morgan and the infantry of Jackson and Hood. The blood of the old men stirred to the distant breath of battle; the blood of the young men leaped hot with eager desire to accompany us. The older women, who remembered the dreadful misery of war—the misery that presses its iron weight most heavily on the wives and the little ones—looked sadly at us; but the young girls drove down in bevies,

A staff meeting with General Wheeler of the cavalry division. (AdeQHA)

arrayed in their finery, to wave flags in farewell to the troopers and to beg cartridges and buttons as mementos. Everywhere we saw the Stars and Stripes, and everywhere we were told, half-laughing, by grizzled ex-Confederates that they had never dreamed in the bygone days of bitterness to greet the old flag as they now were greeting it, and to send their sons, as now they were sending them, to fight and die under it.

Religion and race

The majority of 19th-century America was Protestant, ranging from Anglican, Baptist, and Methodist, to Quaker, Presbyterian, and other evangelist groups. Roman Catholicism was still strongly present in the Hispanic communities of the southwest and Gulf states as well as in immigrant communities such as the Irish and Poles. Another significant immigrant group comprised those from Eastern Europe, who brought with them Judaism.

The Reverend Henry A. Brown of Prescott, Arizona became the regimental chaplain of the 1st United States Volunteer Cavalry. On Sundays both before and during the campaign, he held mass for the troopers. Throughout the campaign, Reverend Brown helped ease the toils of war experienced by his spiritual charges. After their first battle at Las Guásimas on June 24, 1898, Roosevelt noted:

> Next morning we buried seven dead Rough Riders in a grave on the summit of the trail. Chaplain Brown reading the solemn burial service of the Episcopalians, while the men stood around with bared heads and joined in singing, "Rock of Ages."

In the United States of the 19th and mid-20th centuries the predominant view was that the white Anglo-Saxon protestant was at the top of the economic and social ladder while white Anglo-Saxon non-Protestant immigrants (such as Irish Catholics) were below, with Hispanics/Latinos, Chinese, American Indians, and African-Americans on the bottom rungs. Roosevelt was proud of the diversity of men within the ranks of the 1st United States Volunteer Cavalry. He wrote:

> The regiment attracted adventurous spirits from everywhere. Our chief trumpeter was a native American, our second trumpeter was from the Mediterranean—

I think an Italian—who had been a soldier of fortune not only in Egypt, but in the French Army in Southern China. Two excellent men were Osborne, a tall Australian, who had been an officer in the New South Wales Mounted Rifles; and Cook, an Englishman, who had served in South Africa.

Roosevelt showed a keen interest in the different members of the regiment that were of American Indian heritage. He observed:

Only a few were of pure blood. The others shaded off until they were absolutely indistinguishable from their white comrades; with whom, it may be mentioned, they all lived on terms of complete equality ... Not all of the Indians were from the Indian Territory. One of the gamest fighters and best soldiers in the regiment was Pollock, a full-blooded Pawnee. He had been educated, like most of the other Indians, at one of those admirable Indian schools which have added so much to the total of the small credit account with which the White race balances the very unpleasant debit account of its dealings with the Red. Pollock was a silent, solitary fellow—an excellent penman, much given to drawing pictures. When we got down to Santiago he developed into the regimental clerk. I never suspected him of having a sense of humor until one day, at the end of our stay in Cuba, as he was sitting in the Adjutant's tent working over the returns, there turned up a trooper of the First who had been acting as barber. Eying him with immovable face Pollock asked, in a guttural voice: "Do you cut hair?" The man answered "Yes"; and Pollock continued, "Then you'd better cut mine," muttering, in an explanatory soliloquy: "Don't want to wear my hair long like a wild Indian when I'm in civilized warfare."

African-Americans faced a tougher life in the United States at the turn of the 19th century. During the reconstruction period following the Civil War, the federal government of the United States briefly provided some civil rights protection in the south for African-Americans, the majority of whom had been enslaved by white owners. When reconstruction abruptly ended in 1877, and federal troops were withdrawn, southern state governments passed laws prohibiting black people from using the same public facilites as whites, and prohibited whites from hiring black workers for all but the most menial jobs, a situation that created severe economic hardship for the families of black workers. The "Jim Crow laws," named for a familiar minstrel character of the day, also required black and white people to use separate water fountains, public schools, public bathhouses, restaurants, public libraries, and railcars in

"War is over!" Rough Riders cheer the news that the Spanish garrison in Santiago has capitulated, July 17, 1898. (AdeQHA)

public transport. The 1890s also saw resurgent racism in the north. These factors increased the segregation of blacks from whites, culminating in the Plessy vs. Ferguson decision by the Supreme Court in 1896 that codified the "separate but equal" doctrine into law.

Despite the prejudices against African-Americans, those whites that fought alongside colored troops shared a different opinion. Rough Rider Carl Lovelace, writing to the *Waco Times Herald*, stated:

> One thing I noticed; one great thing; one thing, that if the colonial policy is adopted by our people, ought to be a large factor in solving the ever recurring race problem. Get it out of your head that Negroes can't fight. They can. That Tenth cavalry. Will I ever forget one charge I saw them make. They were on our left, and in taking one hill, moved out about two minutes before we did. Amidst a hail of bullets I saw them deploy and move up the hill as if on dress parade with a grand stand attachment. At every step some of them fell but the line never even wavered. They simply closed up to all the gaps, and kept advancing, shooting and cheering as they went. We made some good charges ourselves, but we don't make them with the exquisite mechanical perfection of the Tenth Cavalry Colored. They surprised us all, and I've got more respect for the colored soldier and citizen than I ever had before. [Lovelace 1898, Letter Four]

Roosevelt provides some details in his memoirs of Hispanic American experiences during the war. With regard to the volunteering of a Captain Maximilian Luna of New Mexico, he wrote:

> The Captain's people had been on the banks of the Rio Grande before my forefathers came to the mouth of the Hudson or Wood's landed at Plymouth; and he made the plea that it was his right to go as a representative of his race, for he was the only man of pure Spanish blood who bore a commission in the army, and he demanded the privilege of proving that his people were precisely as loyal Americans as any others. I was glad when it was decided to take him.

The American military grew to respect the Spanish enemy troops they encountered during the campaign and the senior officers of both armies extended courtesies to each other. The common view amongst these officers

ABOVE LEFT
Conditions steadily worsened in the camps of the 1st United States Volunteer Cavalry and other American units. Plans were implemented to return these men as soon as possible to the United States before diseases took their toll. On August 6 the Rough Riders boarded their transport for their trip to Montauk, New York. (AdeQHA)

ABOVE RIGHT
Sergeant Wright with the regimental flag of the 1st United States Volunteer Cavalry Regiment presented by the Women's Relief Corps. (AdeQHA)

was that as professional soldiers there were certain codes of behavior that should be respected. One Rough Rider, Francis M. McArty, noted:

> With the Spaniards we were favorably impressed. After the fighting they were extremely courteous and when we went where they were it seemed like they were constantly exerting themselves to do something for us. [McArty 1898, p. 1]

However, the American view of the Cuban insurgents that began their third war of independence in 1895 was somewhat different. These troops formed a ragged but fiercely proud fighting force. The Cubans were of mixed creole, mulatto, and/or black race. Roosevelt penned the following comments on the Cuban rebels he encountered upon landing at Daiquirí:

> There had been [a] number of Spaniards at Daiquirí that morning, but they had fled even before the ships began shelling. In their place we found hundreds of Cuban insurgents, a crew of as utter tatterdemalions as human eyes ever looked on, armed with every kind of rifle in all stages of dilapidation. It was evident, at a glance, that they would be no use in serious fighting, but it was hoped that they might be of service in scouting. From a variety of causes, however, they turned out to be nearly useless, even for this purpose, so far as the Santiago campaign was concerned.

Francis M. McArty, a member of Troop A, Teddy Roosevelt's Rough Riders, was even more opinionated about the Cubans:

> Would I enlist again in case of further trouble in Cuba? No, I don't think I would to fight the Spanish, but if I got a chance to go back to whip those dirty, thieving Cubans, who will neither fight nor work, I think that I would embrace the opportunity. That is the way I feel about the Cubans. We have no use for them … They are absolutely no good except to feed. They are a full hand at that. They would not fight and would not work. At first we gave them full rations and when we learned what kind of cattle they were we quit. Then they stole from us, taking anything we had, clothing, blankets, tents or anything that they could

get their hands on. They are absolutely worthless, and it is my firm belief that they will give this country trouble. The Cubans are made up of whites, negroes and half-breeds and are more ignorant than the American negro. Garcia's army was composed of the rag-tag and bob-tail element. Some of them looked like they were not more than 12 years old and others looked like they were 80. Caste is very strictly observed on the island. First the white Cuban is taken and after him the full-blooded negro. The half-breeds are at the bottom of the scale. The people there have but little use for the half-breed. [McArty 1898, p.1]

These biased opinions were shared by General Shafter too; following the surrender of Santiago de Cuba by the Spaniards to the Americans, Shafter barred the Cuban insurgents and their leaders from participating in the ceremonies.

At least one Rough Rider did recognize and praise the Cubans for their efforts to assist the Americans during the Santiago campaign. Sergeant John J. Turner, who served in Troop D, wrote of their commanding generals:

A Rough Rider memorial in Arlington National Cemetery. Numerous memorials and historical markers dedicated to the famous regiment are to be found wherever they set foot in the United States. (AdeQHA)

There are many authorities who omit entirely the part played by the Cuban forces in the landing of the Americans and capture of the most important positions around Santiago. These Generals with their forces left Asserradero in the following manner for Daiquirí Siboney: General Francisco Sanchez on board the *Leone*, General Jose M. Capote on the *Seneca*, General Agustin Cebreco on the *Drijaba*, and General Garcia with Generals Jesus Rabi, Saturnino Lora, Rafael Portuondo with their staff on the *Alamo* with General William Ludlow. The above mentioned were men of great prestige, the majority of them having fought in the war between Spaniards and Cubans from 1868 to 1878, or in other words the ten years war. [Turner 1918]

Colonel Roosevelt and his Rough Riders attending the first reunion in Las Vegas, Nevada, 1899. (AdeQHA)

LIFE ON CAMPAIGN

Prior to leaving Tampa in Florida for Cuba, the Rough Riders were brigaded with the 1st and 10th (colored) Regular Cavalry under Brigadier General S. B. M. Young, to form the 2nd Brigade. The 1st Brigade consisted of the 3rd, 6th, and 9th (colored) Regular Cavalry under Brigadier General Sumner. Both these brigades of the cavalry division came under the command of Major General Joseph Wheeler, who had commanded the Confederate cavalry during the Civil War. The cavalry division was part of the US Fifth Corps.

At Port Tampa, things were in great disarray, with Fifth Corps in a highly disorganized state. In the confusion of embarkation, several regiments were assigned to the same transport, the *Yucatan* (also known as Transport No. 8). Roosevelt got his men aboard, realizing that, once aboard, they would probably not be forced to disembark. The Rough Riders stayed there, much to the chagrin of the other regiments. Because of a lack of room in the army transports, only eight of the regiment's twelve troops (A, B, D, E, F, G, K, and L) went to Cuba, with the other four troops (C, H, I, and M) remaining behind in Florida to care for the regiment's horses (which were almost all left behind) and equipment. The Rough Riders had essentially become an infantry regiment. The troopers waited in the steel hulks of the transports for nearly two weeks, until the ship finally embarked for Cuba on June 14. Many of the men were unaccustomed to sailing on the open seas. Sharing much of the same experience as his comrades, Private Carl Lovelace wrote about the journey to Cuba in a letter dated June 20, 1898:

> At daybreak we rounded Cape Maceo and are now headed to the west. Our destination we don't exactly know, but think we are to land at a point about forty miles west of Santiago. We are now making very slow time and it will be

late tomorrow before we get off this infernal ship. I have been sea sick, in fact I am still sea sick, and I yearn for the solid earth, with a yearning that can't be stilled. I have spent the last twenty-four hours at the railing, and am now as hollow as any mockery on earth.

Early this morning, when I awoke, my eyes rested on a grayish mass to the north, it was Cuba, and a tumult of emotions raged through me. Because there before me was the enchanted isle of song and story; there the spot where liberty struggles as in her birth throes and freedom seems to be fading from the great world's face? O, nein – it was because there were good solid earth – ground – you understand – God-given dirt, that you could put your foot on in one place without having a place five feet in front of you caress you on your alabaster brow.

You don't understand, you can never understand, until you are on the sea about four days. What a magnificent thing was God's flat. "Let there be land." Sick – why I have thrown up every thing except my job, and only the iron-clad oath Uncle Sam administers enabled me to hold that. But the voyage is nearly over now, and midst the fire and smoke of conflict, which soon will come, all this will be forgotten.

Several movies and documentaries ha ve been made on the Rough Riders. This 1928 still is simply entitled "Rough Riders." In 1998 TNT produced another, though highly inaccurate, film of the same name. (AdeQHA)

We are going almost due west now, under a pretty fair head of steam, and by tomorrow any way, will land. Whether we will have any trouble in landing is a thing we don't know. [Lovelace 1898, Letter One]

A "hot time" on the march

The men of the 1st United States Volunteer Cavalry landed near Daiquirí, Cuba on June 22. Roosevelt described the sequence of events as the men and equipment were unloaded from the *Yucatan*:

On landing we spent some active hours in marching our men a quarter of a mile or so inland, as boat-load by boat-load they disembarked. We were camped on a dusty, brush-covered flat, with jungle on one side, and on the other a shallow, fetid pool fringed with palm-trees. Huge land-crabs scuttled noisily through the underbrush, exciting much interest among the men. Camping was a simple matter, as each man carried all he had, and the officers had nothing. I took a light mackintosh and a tooth-brush. Fortunately, that night it did not rain; and from the palm-leaves we built shelters from the sun.

The Rough Riders then began marching towards their objective of Santiago de Cuba. Campaign life proved hard for the men of the 1st United States Volunteer Cavalry. In his diary entry dated June 23, Private Roger S. Fitch noted:

About 4 p.m. started for Siboney about 8 miles en route for Santiago. Arr. about 8 p.m. Hard march—hot!—over the hills with about 70 lbs. of "stuff" on our backs. [Fitch 1997, p. 195]

The men were not prepared for the tropical climate of Cuba, and nor were they in good shape for marching, having been used to traveling everywhere by horse. Between marches and skirmishes with the Spaniards, the Rough Riders spent much of their time clearing land, setting camps, erecting bombproofs, and digging trenches. Roosevelt noted his men's positive attitude, despite the conditions:

The heat was intense and their burdens very heavy. Yet there was very little straggling. Whenever we halted they instantly took off their packs and threw themselves on their backs. Then at the word to start they would spring into place again. The captains and lieutenants tramped along, encouraging the men by example and word. A good part of the time I was by Captain Llewellen, and was greatly pleased to see the way in which he kept his men up to their work. He never pitied or coddled his troopers, but he always looked after them. He helped them whenever he could, and took rather more than his full share of hardship and danger, so that his men naturally followed him with entire devotion. Jack Greenway was under him as lieutenant, and to him the entire march was nothing but an enjoyable outing, the chance of fight on the morrow simply adding the needed spice of excitement.

Rough Rider collectables are rare and can command high prices. Pictured are General Leonard Wood's sword presented to him by the men of Company A, 9th Regiment Massachusetts Volunteer Militia; the Rough Rider Medal presented by Colonel Roosevelt; and various hat insignia attributed to the regiment. (AdeQHA)

Disease

A total of 2,446 men out of the 306,760 who served in Cuba died. Only 385 of these deaths were combat related, the majority of the remaining 2,061 being caused by sickness and disease (approximately 20 Rough Riders died of disease during the war). The biggest killers were malaria, dysentery, and typhoid. The latter, however, was highly prevalent among troops that remained in the United States too. A commission under Major Walter Reed, formed to investigate the origin and spread of typhoid fever in United States military camps during the Spanish-American War, stated the following findings in its 1904 report:

(1) During the Spanish War of 1898 every regiment constituting the First, Second, Third, Fourth, Fifth, and Seventh Army Corps developed typhoid fever.

(2) More than 90 per cent of the volunteer regiments developed typhoid fever within eight weeks after going into camp...

D **TRENCH WARFARE**
After they had been in Cuba for some time, the men of the 1st United States Volunteer Cavalry Regiment began to feel the effects of campaigning in the tropical conditions. Constant marching, intermingled with the odd skirmish with the Spaniards, progressed into the rigors of trench warfare for the Rough Riders, as shown in this illustration. The men were constantly harassed by Spanish artillery and enemy snipers armed with Mauser rifles. To add to their woes, diseases such as malaria, typhoid, and dysentery wrought havoc on the soldiers of General Shafter's 5th Army Corps, of which the Rough Riders were a part.

ABOVE LEFT
Colonel Roosevelt, portrayed by Michael Caweti, with extras portraying Spanish soldiers on the set of "The Spanish-American War: First Intervention." (Author's photo)

ABOVE RIGHT
A Rough Rider with full kit including a Collins #22 machete. (AdeQHA)

(15) Camp pollution was the greatest sin committed by the troops in 1898…

(45) About one-fifth of the soldiers in the national encampments in the United States in 1898 developed typhoid fever…

(47) The percentage of death among cases of typhoid fever was 7.61. [Reed 1904, pp. 656, 663, 674, 675]

Those Rough Riders left behind in Tampa suffered tremendously as Roosevelt noted in his memoirs:

> The men who had remained at Tampa, like ourselves, had suffered much from fever, and the horses were in bad shape. So many of the men were sick that none of the regiments began to drill for some time after reaching Montauk.

For comparison sake, the 2nd United States Volunteer Cavalry (known as "Torrey's Rough Riders") was decimated while encamped in Jacksonville, Florida, as the 1904 report makes clear:

> Surgeon Jessurun states on the September report of sick and wounded that the prevailing diseases have been typhoid fever, acute diarrhea, and a form of malarial remittent fever of atypical character. He also says that the diarrheas were very obstinate, not being controlled by medication. For this month, in an average strength of 796 officers and men, we find 426 admissions, divided as follows: Acute diarrhea, 180; remittent fever, 145; typhoid fever, 63; all other causes, 38. [Reed 1904, p. 626]

Large numbers of men from the 1st United States Volunteer Cavalry suffered from a variety of diseases as well as heat exhaustion during the campaign in Cuba. After the fall of Santiago, Roosevelt wrote the following on the condition of his men prior to their return to the United States:

> Yellow fever also broke out in the rear, chiefly among the Cubans. It never became epidemic, but it caused a perfect panic among some of our own doctors, and especially in the minds of one or two generals and of the home authorities. We found that whenever we sent a man to the rear he was decreed to have

yellow fever, whereas, if we kept him at the front, it always turned out that he had malarial fever, and after a few days he was back at work again. I doubt if there were ever more than a dozen genuine cases of yellow fever in the whole cavalry division; but the authorities at Washington, misled by the reports they received from one or two of their military and medical advisers at the front, became panic-struck, and under the influence of their fears hesitated to bring the army home, lest it might import yellow fever into the United States. Their panic was absolutely groundless, as shown by the fact that when brought home not a single case of yellow fever developed upon American soil. Our real foe was not the yellow fever at all, but malarial fever, which was not infectious, but which was certain, if the troops were left throughout the summer in Cuba, to destroy them, either killing them outright, or weakening them so that they would have fallen victims to any disease that attacked them.

EXPERIENCE OF BATTLE

Two days after having landed in Cuba, and whilst marching toward Santiago de Cuba, the Rough Riders would have their first taste of battle. The regiment had only been raised two months previously, and the men now found themselves in a foreign land and were expected to prove themselves against the more combat-experienced Spanish regular and irregular troops. Private Carl Lovelace of Troop D described the build-up to the battle in the following letter dated June 24:

Yesterday was an eventful day. Today promises to be more so, because from my coconut palm tent I can see a grim black looking mountain and on its brow floats the banner of Spain. We are momentarily expecting an order to move. Three regiments of regulars have already moved. The insurgents have been fighting all day, only a few miles from us. Every once in a while I can hear the

LEFT
The Rough Rider Medal presented to the men of the 1st United States Volunteer Cavalry by Colonel Theodore Roosevelt. Many are inscribed on the back with the name and troop of the wearer. (AdeQHA)

RIGHT
Rough Rider memorabilia from the 1900 reunion in Oklahoma City. Of interest is the invitation and special khaki cloth envelope in the form of a uniform breast pocket. (AdeQHA)

A memorial dedicated to the Rough Riders in Arlington Cemetery. (AdeQHA)

roar of some of our warships' guns firing at what is supposed to be a masked battery on the heights around the bay or Santiago. The situation is at least interesting. The scent of battle is in the air and the light of battle gleams in every eye. We are camped thirty miles from Santiago, 200 yards from the Caribbean sea, and in a camp where the Spaniards took breakfast yesterday morning. [Lovelace 1895, Letter Two]

The Battle of Las Guásimas took place the following day. The Spaniards occupied a range of high hills in the form of an obtuse angle, the salient being toward the space between them and the American forces; they also had advance parties located along both roads leading towards Santiago de Cuba. On the part of the ridge where the two trails came together there were stone breastworks flanked by blockhouses. The American troops were slightly outnumbered by the Spanish forces present. Private Carl Lovelace takes up the build up to the bloodying of the Rough Riders:

Friday, June 25, the order to go forward did come. We moved eight miles to a little Spanish town which was abandoned two hours before our arrival. We camped there in the rain, and early yesterday morning went on as the vanguard of the army. About 8 o'clock we ran into an ambush [the Battle of Las Guásimas], and for two hours and twenty-five minutes our regiment was under fire from a hidden enemy. My troop was under fire for about an hour, and bullets fairly rained about us, and into some of us. It was mean fighting, because we couldn't see what to shoot at. The underbrush is so dense that one can hardly see twenty feet in front of him, and where there is no underbrush, the grass is three or four feet high. The country is mountainous and full of ravines. We were dead tired and altogether we had a hard time. Our regiment lost about thirty-one killed and wounded. Capt. Capron of L was killed, his first lieutenant was wounded and Major Brodie of our squad was wounded. Our troop had one slightly and five severely, but not fatally, wounded. I don't understand why more of us were not hit. The bullets seemed to hit everywhere, except in the particular spot where a man was, so it seemed to each man. But we licked the Spaniards. Less than 600 Rough Riders held them off for two hours and a half, then a couple of regiments of regulars came up and they retreated in a hurry. Don't think there is a pleasurable thrill about a long fight; that there is a wild kind of joy about the music of whistling bullets. There isn't. After firing the first half dozen shots the whole thing seemed just like regular routine business, just like marching and drilling and roll call, and all such wearisome things. But I think this was largely due to the fact that we were so tired after our long forced march. When it comes to fighting the Rough Riders are all right. Part of the time we were under two fires, front and flank, and could not see what to shoot at, and still not a man wavered. [Lovelace 1895, Letter Two]

Despite being outnumbered, the American contingent was nonetheless able to force a retreat of the Spanish troops to the city of Santiago. Roosevelt noted the manner of his men during their first experience under sustained fire in the fight at Las Guásimas:

The Spaniards were firing high and for the most part by volleys, and their shooting was not very good, which perhaps was not to be wondered at, as they were a long way off. Gradually, however, they began to get the range and occasionally one of our men would crumple up. In no case did the man make any outcry when hit, seeming to take it as a matter of course; at the outside, making only such a remark as: "Well, I got it that time." With hardly an exception, there was no sign of flinching. I say with hardly an exception, for though I personally did not see an instance, and though all the men at the front behaved excellently, yet there were a very few men who lagged behind and drifted back to the trail over which we had come. The character of the fight put a premium upon such conduct, and afforded a very severe test for raw troops; because the jungle was so dense that as we advanced in open order, every man was, from time to time, left almost alone and away from the eyes of his officers. There was unlimited opportunity for dropping out without attracting notice, while it was peculiarly hard to be exposed to the fire of an unseen foe, and to see men dropping under it, and yet to be, for some time, unable to return it, and also to be entirely ignorant of what was going on in any other part of the field.

A Rough Rider in the uniform of the United Spanish War Veterans wearing the regimental medal presented by Colonel Roosevelt. (AdeQHA)

Francis M. McArty described further how the common man reacted while in combat, and the dangers faced:

I can hardly say how a man feels when in action or what he thinks about. The fact is you don't have time to think. Your consuming ambition is to get at the enemy and you lose sight of everything else. When a man fell we stopped to see if he was wounded or dead. If wounded we did what we could to make him comfortable. If dead we mentally said "Another poor fellow gone, may be my turn next," and pushed on. I escaped without a wound but had one close call before Santiago. A bullet hit a tree and rebounding struck me between the shoulders as I was lying on the ground. I felt like some one had thrown a base ball at me with all their strength. I really thought that I had been shot through, but a colored soldier next to me told me not to worry, that there was plenty of fight left in me. For a week or more there was a black and blue spot on my back as big as a silver dollar. On the 2nd of July a shell passed just over me. There were three lines back of the trenches, the lines being about twenty paces apart. The shell struck the ground in front of the second line, bounded up and exploded over the third line, killing three men. The shell came from the fleet in the bay, and the aim of the gunners was accurate. The Spanish had a tremendous advantage over us in being able to see the smoke of our black powder, while their smokeless powder made it difficult for us to locate them. [McCarty 1898]

The Battle of San Juan Heights

On July 1, 1898 the battle began with Captain Grime's battery firing from El Pozo Hill upon the Spanish defenses on San Juan Heights. During the course of the morning some of the officers grew impatient of waiting for orders, including Colonel Theodore Roosevelt. His dismounted cavalry lay waiting in trenches at the base of the hill, suffering casualties to enemy fire as they remained there. In the absence of orders, Roosevelt took it upon himself to lead a bold charge. Facing the Rough Riders was a smaller hill, which received the name Kettle Hill because of the presence of a large kettle near its base. Roosevelt formed up his regiment and began to move forward. However, the Rough Riders' advance began to slow as troops dropped from heat exhaustion. The colonel feared that he could not keep up on foot in the tropical heat and instead stayed mounted. Soon officers from the rest of Wood's brigade along with Carrol's brigade began to advance, and the units became intermingled. One of the units involved was the 10th United States (colored) Cavalry. The attackers eventually cut their way through barbed wire entanglements near the top of the hill and drove the Spaniards out of their trenches on Kettle Hill.

At the same moment Brigadier General Hamilton Hawkins' brigade was faring no better than Roosevelt had in his original position. Lieutenant Jule G. Ord of the 6th United States Infantry rushed to the front of the brigade. With Ord leading, the brigade moved out of the trenches and advanced up the slope. One hundred and fifty yards from the hill the troops charged, cutting their way through the barbed wire. Seeing the spontaneous advances of Colonel Roosevelt and Lieutenant Ord, Wheeler gave the order for Brigadier General Jacob Ford Kent to advance with his whole division while he returned to the Cavalry Division. Kent sent forward Ewers' brigade to join Hawkins' men, who were already approaching the hill. Kent's men discovered

THE BATTLE OF KETTLE HILL
The moment of glory for the Rough Riders came when Colonel Roosevelt and his men charged up the San Juan Heights and took Kettle Hill on July 1, 1898. The heat was incredible during the battle and many of the men were overcome by heat exhaustion during the charge. Despite the hardship and losses endured by Roosevelt's men in the initial charge, they managed to garner enough strength to charge down Kettle Hill and then up the next hill, thereby capturing the entire ridge of the San Juan Heights.

Newly recruited Rough Riders being given a send-off by the locals. (AdeQHA)

that the Spanish had placed their trenches in faulty positions and that his men were actually covered from the fire of the Spaniards as they climbed the hill. Lieutenant Ord, still in the lead, was among the first to reach the crest. The Spanish troops fled, but as Ord jumped into the trench he was killed instantly, and Hawkins was wounded shortly after.

After losing Kettle Hill, the Spaniards that were still on San Juan Hill began to fire on the Rough Riders' newly won position. While General Kent's men secured a blockhouse to the south after hand-to-hand fighting, Sumner also charged San Juan Hill. Roosevelt personally led the attack, but paused after charging a few feet with only a handful of men following. He turned around and enquired why no one had followed. His men replied they had not heard the order and quickly joined the attack. General Kent's remaining brigade under Colonel E. P. Pearson arrived after General Hawkins had already charged and moved farther to the south, and drove the Spanish off a knoll on the Spanish right flank.

Francis M. McArty witnessed Roosevelt during the heat of battle and recounted the following details:

Roosevelt was adored by his men. The stories of his gallant riding up and down the line are not so. He had an old mule, but at San Juan when we struck a barbed wire fence he dismounted and tied the beast and led us on foot. About his personal bravery there is no question. He was up in the front cheering us. He is not foolhardy. He calculates his chances and takes advantage of it. If it remained with his regiment he would be the governor of New York and no questions asked. With his men he was just familiar enough to show them that he appreciated their services. He knew them personally and called them by name, but in a way that always left the opinion that a man could go so far with him, but no farther. He roughed it with us and underwent the same hardships that we did. General Joe Wheeler is another man whom we idolized. He is a fighter. [McArty 1898, p.1]

The following account of an incident observed during the Battle of San Juan Heights involving the Rough Riders' dynamite gun is an interesting one. The account was written by Richard Harding Davis, the foremost war correspondent of the era; the "Sgt. Borrowe" he refers to is actually Sergeant Burrowe:

> I came upon Sergeant Borrowe blocking the road with his dynamite gun. He and his brother and three regulars were busily correcting a hitch in its mechanism. An officer carrying an order along the line halted his sweating horse and gazed at the strange gun with professional knowledge. "That must be the dynamite gun I have heard so much about," he shouted. Borrowe saluted and shouted assent. The officer, greatly interested, forgot his errand. "I'd like to see you fire it once," he said eagerly. Borrowe, delighted at the chance to exhibit his toy to a professional soldier, beamed with equal eagerness. "In just a moment, sir," he said; "this shell seems to have jammed a bit." The officer, for the first time seeing the shell stuck in the breech, hurriedly gathered up his reins. He seemed to be losing interest. With elaborate carelessness I began to edge off down the road. "Wait," Borrowe begged, "we'll have it out in a minute." Suddenly I heard the officer's voice raised wildly. "What—what," he gasped, "is that man doing with that axe ?" "He's helping me to get out this shell," said Borrowe. "Good God!" said the officer. Then he remembered his errand. Until last year, when I again met young Borrowe gayly disporting himself at a lawn-tennis tournament at Mattapoisett, I did not know whether his brother's method of removing dynamite with an axe had been entirely successful. He said it worked all right. [Davis 1910, pp. 123–24]

Roosevelt recalled the bravery and bravado of one Rough Rider during the attack on the Spanish defenses on San Juan Heights, an episode that has become part of the regiment's lore:

Former Confederate General "Fightin' Joe" Wheeler became commander of the Cavalry Division of which the 1st United States Volunteer Cavalry was part. Standing next to him are Colonel Wood and Lieutenant Colonel Roosevelt. (AdeQHA)

The most serious loss that I and the regiment could have suffered befell just before we charged. Bucky O'Neill was strolling up and down in front of his men, smoking his cigarette, for he was inveterately addicted to the habit. He had a theory that an officer ought never to take cover—a theory which was, of course, wrong, though in a volunteer organization the officers should certainly expose themselves very fully, simply for the effect on the men; our regimental toast on the transport running, "The officers; may the war last until each is killed, wounded, or promoted." As O'Neill moved to and fro, his men begged him to lie down, and one of the sergeants said, "Captain, a bullet is sure to hit you." O'Neill took his cigarette out of his mouth, and blowing out a cloud of smoke laughed and said, 'Sergeant, the Spanish bullet isn't made that will kill me." A little later he discussed for a moment with one of the regular officers the direction from which the Spanish fire was coming. As he turned on his heel a bullet struck him in the mouth and came out at the back of his head; so that even before he fell his wild and gallant soul had gone out into the darkness.

The final road to victory

Immediately after their victory in the Battle of San Juan Heights, the Rough Riders began occupying and refurbishing the Spanish defenses they had captured, which now afforded them a view of Santiago. General Wood sent requests for Kent to send up infantry to strengthen his vulnerable position. General Wheeler reached the trenches and ordered breastworks constructed. Roosevelt's men did in fact repulse a minor counterattack on the northern flank. The Americans' position on San Juan Hill was exposed to artillery fire from within Santiago; Shafter feared the vulnerability of the line, and ordered the troops to withdraw. Wheeler assured Shafter that the position could be held; yet Shafter still ordered the withdrawal. Before the men could pull back, Wheeler called aside Kent and Sumner and reassured them that the line could be held, and during the night they worked at strengthening the lines while reinforcements arrived.

The taking of the hills did not mean that the men were clear of danger. Spanish snipers still preyed upon those who were visible from their trenches, and in return a few selected men from the Rough Riders sniped on the Spaniards. Within days, the Spanish fleet of Admiral Cervera was destroyed as it attempted to break out of Santiago Harbor on 3 July. General José Toral, commander of the Spanish forces in Santiago, had no other choice but to surrender. Roosevelt remembered the following reaction of his men upon hearing the news:

> On the 17th the city formally surrendered and our regiment, like the rest of the army, was drawn up on the trenches. When the American flag was hoisted the trumpets blared and the men cheered, and we knew that the fighting part of our work was over.

ROOSEVELT SAYS "GOODBYE"
"One afternoon, to my genuine surprise, I was asked out of my tent by Lieutenant-Colonel Brodie (the gallant old boy had rejoined us), and found the whole regiment formed in hollow square, with the officers and color-sergeant in the middle. When I went in, one of the troopers came forward and on behalf of the regiment presented me with Remington's fine bronze, "The Bronco-buster." There could have been no more appropriate gift from such a regiment, and I was not only pleased with it, but very deeply touched with the feeling which made them join in giving it. Afterward they all filed past and I shook the hands of each to say good-by." (Theodore Roosevelt, *The Rough Riders*)

The Rough Riders remained encamped in the San Juan Heights for another month, where living, sanitary, and health conditions continued to worsen by the day. To break the monotony of life in the camp, many of the troopers ventured into Santiago to see the sites and barter with the locals for cigars, rum, and items of food.

AFTERMATH

The Rough Riders returned to Montauk, New York on August 14, 1898 and the regiment spent a month in quarantine. Colonel Roosevelt recalled the atmosphere there:

> The last night before we were mustered out was spent in noisy, but entirely harmless hilarity, which I ignored. Every form of celebration took place in the ranks. A former Populist candidate for Attorney-General in Colorado delivered a fervent oration in favor of free silver; a number of the college boys sang; but most of the men gave vent to their feelings by improvised dances. In these the Indians took the lead, pure bloods and half-breeds alike, the cowboys and miners cheerfully joining in and forming part of the howling, grunting rings, that went bounding around the great fires they had kindled.

> Next morning Sergeant Wright took down the colors, and Sergeant Guitilias the standard, for the last time; the horses, the rifles, and the rest of the regimental property had been turned in; officers and men shook hands and said good-by to one another, and then they scattered to their homes in the North and the South, the few going back to the great cities of the East, the many turning again toward the plains, the mountains, and the deserts of the West and the strange Southwest. This was on September 15th, the day which marked the close of the four months' life of a regiment of as gallant fighters as ever wore the United States uniform.

At the onset of hostilities with Spain the muster roll of the Rough Riders consisted of the 47 officers and 994 enlisted men. The tally for mustering out was 76 officers and 1,090 enlisted men, and the total number accounted for on the muster out roll was 52 officers, 1,185 enlisted men. The difference in numbers of the officers and troopers from onset to mustering out reflects the addition of new recruits as the regiment moved towards Florida from New Mexico, consolidation of companies left in Tampa with the regiment's arrival in Montauk, as well as transfers to and from other regiments or assignments. The latter is one such case where General Leonard Wood and a few officers from the regiment were assigned to operate the new military government being established in Cuba.

The losses while in service were as follows: total officer losses were 5 (resigned or discharged, 2; killed in action, 2; died of disease, 1); total enlisted men losses were 95 (discharged for disability, 9; discharged by order, 31; killed in action, 21; died of wounds received in action, 3; died of disease, 19; suicide, 14; deserted, 12). The tallies for the number of wounded were 7 officers and 97 enlisted men. Virgil Carrington Jones, in his book *Roosevelt's Rough Riders* (1971), writes of Roosevelt's regiment:

In the period of about four and a half months they were together, 37 percent of those who got to Cuba were casualties. Better than one out of every three were killed, wounded, or stricken by disease. It was the highest casualty rate of any American unit that took part in the Spanish-American War campaign.

Most of the Rough Riders returned to their previous lives without issues or problems. Some even managed to benefit from their exploits. Roosevelt became governor of New York and later President of the United States, Leonard Wood became the military governor of Cuba, and Frank Frantz became governor of the Oklahoma Territory. Roosevelt wrote of the pride his men had for the work that they had done and the sacrifices they had made, and how this translated into support and aid for those that had suffered misfortune during the war:

> When we were mustered out, many of the men had lost their jobs, and were too weak to go to work at once, while there were helpless dependents of the dead to care for. Certain of my friends, August Belmont, Stanley and Richard Mortimer, Major Austin Wadsworth—himself fresh from the Manila campaign—Belmont Tiffany, and others, gave me sums of money to be used for helping these men. In some instances, by the exercise of a good deal of tact and by treating the gift as a memorial of poor young Lieutenant Tiffany, we got the men to accept something; and, of course, there were a number who, quite rightly, made no difficulty about accepting. But most of the men would accept no help whatever.

On the way to Cuba, Captain Buckey O'Neill had suggested that the Military Order of the Morro be formed to keep Rough Riders in touch after the war. In August 1898, as the regiment prepared to be discharged, the Roosevelt Rough Rider Association took shape, with Brodie as president and Roosevelt and Wood as vice-presidents. They agreed to meet in annual reunions.

The first annual reunion was held at Las Vegas, New Mexico, in June of 1899; the second in Oklahoma City; the third in Colorado Springs; and the fourth at San Antonio. In addition to socializing, the former Rough Riders pledged to help each other find employment and get out of difficulties. In 1905 they chipped in to buy an artificial leg for Private Charles Buckholdt who had lost his own in a bar fight. There were no official regimental reunions from 1905 until 1948, when the former Rough Riders met in Prescott to commemorate the 50th anniversary of the Battle of Las Guásimas. Some 65 of the 107 surviving veterans attended. From 1949 through 1968 annual reunions took place in Las Vegas, New Mexico.

Through the decades that followed the war, various memorials and historical markers commemorating the 1st United States Volunteer Cavalry were established in the United States in places through which the Rough Riders had passed during the Spanish-American War. On July 3, 1907 a memorial monument was dedicated to Buckey O'Neill and the other Rough Riders in Prescott, Arizona. Seven thousand people gathered to witness the unveiling. Many mistakenly think that the statue is of O'Neill, when in fact it is not. In Arlington National Cemetery is another Rough Rider memorial that commemorates those who died in Cuba. On the top of San Juan Hill, Cuba near a reconstructed Spanish blockhouse, lie memorials to Theodore Roosevelt and his Rough Riders; they remain to this day.

Many regional gatherings did take place of former Rough Riders. One was held in Hollywood in 1928 to launch the movie *Rough Riders*, directed by Victor Fleming. Many Rough Riders also attended the annual meetings of the United Spanish War Veterans, which were open to all who had served in that conflict. Jesse Langdon, the longest surviving member of the Rough Riders, died on June 28, 1975.

A final footnote to the legacy of the Rough Riders occurred on January 16, 2001 when Theodore Roosevelt became the first United States President to posthumously receive the Medal of Honor, the highest award for Military Service given in the United States, for his actions during the Battle of San Juan Hill. The citation read as follows:

> Lieutenant Colonel Theodore Roosevelt distinguished himself by acts of bravery on 1 July 1898, near Santiago de Cuba, Republic of Cuba, while leading a daring charge up San Juan Hill. Lieutenant Colonel Roosevelt, in total disregard for his personal safety, and accompanied by only four or five men, led a desperate and gallant charge up San Juan Hill, encouraging his troops to continue the assault through withering enemy fire over open countryside. Facing the enemy's heavy fire, he displayed extraordinary bravery throughout the charge, and was the first to reach the enemy trenches, where he quickly killed one of the enemy with his pistol, allowing his men to continue the assault. His leadership and valor turned the tide in the Battle for San Juan Hill. Lieutenant Colonel Roosevelt's extraordinary heroism and devotion to duty are in keeping with the highest traditions of military service and reflect great credit upon himself, his unit, and the United States Army.

The Roosevelt family gave the medal back to the White House on September 16, 2002. There are plans to display it in the Roosevelt Room of the White House, along with the Nobel Peace Prize awarded to Roosevelt as President for his efforts to end the Russo-Japanese War of 1904–05.

COLLECTIONS, MUSEUMS, AND LIVING HISTORY

Despite being in existence for only 133 days, the 1st United States Volunteer Cavalry won its place in history, and has since passed into legend. Collecting memorabilia pertaining to the Rough Riders has to be considered a specialized field. The 1st United States Volunteer Cavalry wore standard United States Army equipment and uniforms that differed little from those worn by regulars or state troops. Interested buyers should note that the cap insignia of crossed sabers and a numeral "1" does not indicate that it belonged to a Rough Rider. On many occasions such insignia has been sold as such, often for high prices, without stating that it could have been worn by a trooper from the 1st United States Cavalry (regular army) or even from the 1st New York Cavalry. The emblem must be affixed to a named campaign hat with provenance, and then, and only then, can one consider the emblem "authentic Rough Rider." The rarest of these hat emblems are those procured by the members that have additional designations affixed to the sabers, such as "VOLS" or "USV"—these would have been private purchases, since the majority worn, as evidenced in photographs, were of standard army issue.

Often enough unscrupulous dealers have "created" a fantasy piece using original materials from different sources. On one occasion a United States Army M1898 tropical tunic was mated with buttons of a British City of London Yeomanry unit known as the "Rough Riders." The buttons have a pair of spurs and the letters "RR"—one way to check is to look for a British maker's backmark. The only United States-made buttons on the tunic were a pair of United States Army general service buttons on the breast pockets. This tunic appeared on a popular online auction site, and was being sold as a "Rough Rider's veteran's coat." Sadly, the coat sold to an unsuspecting collector for well over $700 (US). The moral of the tale is—always do your research and/or consult with an expert before making a final decision.

The majority of attributable Rough Rider memorabilia, apart from rare marked uniforms and equipment, are the letters, documents, photographs, stereoviews, and veteran's reunion badges that pop up for sale from time to time. One badge in particular, that is often thought to be a reunion medal, was struck by Theodore Roosevelt for members of the 1st United States Volunteer Cavalry on the unit's return to the United States from Cuba. Roosevelt notes the medal in his book *The Rough Riders*, referring to it as "the medal I gave to my men." It is a two-piece bronze medal with a T-pin top bar entitled "1ST U.S. VOL. CAV." The 5th Corps badge and letters "RR" appear in the center of the planchet, which notes the battles and campaigns of the unit. Occasionally the medal would be inscribed with the name of the recipient.

In addition, though considered rare and a specialized field, collectors sometimes trade in autographs of members of the Rough Riders. A simple signature by General Leonard Wood on a card fetches $300 (US) while a signed first edition copy of *The Rough Riders* by Theodore Roosevelt can fetch $14,000 (US) on the 2009 market.

There are several museums with excellent Rough Rider items within their collections such as the Smithsonian Institution, Sagamore Hill National Historic Site, and Theodore Roosevelt's Birthplace National Historic Site. The Smithsonian has General Leonard Wood's uniform while the latter two have items worn by Roosevelt during the Spanish-American War. Roosevelt's revolver was stolen in 1990 from the Sagamore Hill National Historic Site, but was returned after an absence of 16 years in 2006 and is once more back on display. In addition, the Sharlot Hall Museum (Prescott, Arizona), home of the Arizona Historical Society, has a large collection of artefacts pertaining to the Rough Riders, including some personal effects belonging to Bucky O'Neill. For general collections on the Spanish-American War, the following museums are recommended: The National Infantry Museum (Fort Benning, GA), U.S. Army Quartermaster Museum (Fort Lee, VA), U.S. Cavalry Museum (Fort Riley, KS), Jefferson Barracks (St. Louis, MO), Missouri War Memorial Museum (St. Louis, MO), Tennessee State Museum (Nashville, TN), Indiana War Memorial Museum (Indianapolis, IN), Wisconsin Veterans Museum (Madison, WS), Henry B. Plant Museum (Tampa, FL), Florida State Archives (Tallahassee, FL), Pond Spring—Joseph Wheeler Plantation (Hillsboro, AL), USS Olympia (Philadelphia, PA), and The California State Military Museum (Sacramento, CA).

During the centennial of the Spanish-American War (1998–2002), various living history groups sprang up to portray the 1st United States Volunteer Cavalry. Most of these groups were based in Arizona, California, New Mexico, and Florida. Spanish-American War living history never caught on after the centennial like its counterparts in the American Civil War and World War II. Many of these groups ceased to exist after 2002 with only a few making a comeback for work in the 2005–07 History Channel's production on "The Spanish-American War: First Intervention," a three-hour documentary film. To find existing units that still portray the Rough Riders, one particular website is recommended—The Spanish-American War Centennial Website (www.spanamwar.com) is the oldest and most reliable of websites that provides a valuable tool for living historians and researchers.

BIBLIOGRAPHY

Primary sources

Adjutant General's Office, *Statistical Exhibit of Strength of Volunteer Forces Called Into Service During the War With Spain; with Losses From All Causes,* Washington: Government Printing Office, 1899

Davis, Richard Harding, *Notes of a War Correspondent,* New York: Charles Scribner's Sons, 1910

Fitch, Roger S., U.S.V., "A Rough Rider's Diary" in *The Rough Riders* by Theodore Roosevelt, with additional text by Richard Bak, pp. 194–99, Dallas, TX: Taylor Publishing, 1997

Jacobsen, Jacques Noel (ed.), *Regulations and Notes for the Uniform of the Army of the United States, 1899,* Staten Island, NY: Manor Publishing, 1973 (a reprint of the original uniform regulations)

Leahy, David J., U.S.V., "David Leahy of the First U.S. Volunteer Cavalry ("Rough Riders") Writes Home" *The Raton Range,* 16 June 1898 and 21 July 1898

Lovelace, Carl, U.S.V., "Carl lovelace Writes a Letter/A Waco Boy has been heard from, but it was before the Battle (Letter 1)", *Waco Times Herald,* July 6, 1898, p. 8

—— "Carl Lovelace Tells of the Fight/Letter from a Waco Boy Written near Santiago de Cuba/Heard the Bullets (Letter 2)", *Waco Times Herald,* July 8, 1898, p. 8

—— "Carl Lovelace Writes a Graphic Description of Hot Times around Santiago (Letter 4)", *Waco Times Herald,* August 15, 1898, p. 5

McArty, Francis M., U.S.V., "Francis McArty Talks of The Rough Riders in Cuba", *Herald Dispatch,* Decatur, Illinois, Friday, September 16, 1898

McCurdy, Allen and J. Kirk, U.S.V., "Letters from the McCurdy Brothers" in *Cowboys in Uniform: Uniforms, Arms and Equipment of the Rough Riders,* J.C. Stewart, pp. 11–15, Show Low, AZ: Rough Rider Publishing Co., 1998

"Paying Men in Service", *The New York Times,* 3 July 1898, p. 19

Reed, Walter, Major and Surgeon (U.S. Army), Victor C. Vaughan, Major and Division Surgeon (U.S. Volunteers), and Edward O. Shakespeare, Major and Brigade Surgeon (U.S. Volunteers), *Report of the Origin and Spread of Typhoid Fever in U.S. Military Camps during the Spanish War of 1898,* Washington, DC: Government Printing Office, 1904

Roosevelt, Theodore, *An Autobiography,* New York: Macillan, 1913

—— *The Rough Riders,* New York: Charles Scribner Son's, 1899

Turner, John J., Sgt., U.S.V., "The Campaign in Cuba as Remembered by? Sergeant John J. Turner, U.S.V.", *Beverly Evening Times* (Beverly, Massachusetts), 28 June 1918 (part of this appears on the Spanish-American War Centennial Website, www.spanamwar.com)

Wallace, Alexander H., U.S.V., "A Rough Rider's Story: Alexander H. Wallace's Interesting Letters to His Sister, Mrs. S.F. Johnson", *Brooklyn Eagle,* 29 July 1898

Secondary sources

de Quesada, Alejandro M., "Dress & Field Uniforms of the U.S. Army & State Troops During the Spanish-American War", *Military Trader*, Volume 4, Issue 11 (November 1997): pp. 48–53

—— "The 1895 Forage Cap", *The Military Advisor*, Volume 5, Number 4 (Fall 1994): pp. 4–8

—— *The Spanish American War and Phillipine Insurrection,* Oxford: Osprey Publishing, 2007

—— *The Spanish-American War in Tampa Bay,* Charleston, SC: Arcadia Publishing, 1997

Elting, John R. and Michael McAfee (eds), *Military Uniforms in America,* Volume IV, Novato, CA: Presidio Press, 1988

Flayderman, Norm, *Flayderman's Guide to Antique American Firearms … and their Values* Northbrook, IL: DBI Books, Inc., 1990

Jeffers, H. Paul, *Colonel Roosevelt: Theodore Roosevelt Goes to War, 1897–1898,* New York: John Wiley & Sons, Inc., 1996

Jones, Virgil Carrington, *Roosevelt's Rough Riders,* Garden City, NY: Doubleday & Company, 1971

Henry, Daniel Edward, *Collins' Machetes and Bowies, 1845–1965,* Iola, WI: Krause Publications, 1995

McCurdy, F.A. and J.K., *Two Rough Riders: Letters from F. Allen McCurdy and J. Kirk McCurdy … who Volunteered and Fought with the Rough Riders during the Spanish American War of 1898, to their Father J.M. McCurdy* (private publication, 1902)

Stewart, J.C., *Cowboys in Uniform: Uniforms, Arms and Equipment of the Rough Riders,* Show Low, AZ: Rough Rider Publishing Co., 1998

Walker, Dale L., *The Boys of '98: Theodore Roosevelt and the Rough Riders,* New York: Tom Doherty Associates, Inc., 1998

INDEX